The Call of the Disciple

The Bible on Following Christ

by
Georg Fischer and Martin Hasitschka

Translated by Matthew J. O'Connell

PAULIST PRESS
New York/Mahwah, N.J.

Cover design by Nick Markell

Originally published as *Auf dein Wort hin.* English translation copyright © 1999 by Paulist Press, Inc.

Library of Congress Cataloging-in-Publication Data

Fischer, Georg, 1954–
    [Auf dein Wort hin. English]
    The call of the disciple : the Bible on following Christ / by Georg Fischer and Martin Hasitschka ; translated by Matthew J. O'Connell.
        p.   cm.
    ISBN 0–8091–3858–1 (alk. paper)
    1. Vocation—Biblical teaching. 2. Apostolate (Christian theology)—Biblical teaching. I. Hasitschka, Martin. II. Title.
BS680.V6 F5713 1999
220.9′2—dc21   98–48395
                                                                                CIP

Published by Paulist Press
997 Macarthur Boulevard
Mahwah, New Jersey 07430

www.paulistpress.com

Printed and bound in the
United States of America

Contents

Introduction

*I*t is a glorious spring day in the Alps. The ground is still covered by the remnants of the winter snow, although the rays of the sun are already waking nature to life. Fresh greenery is emerging, crocuses are breaking open a way for themselves, even through ice, into the light.

That is what it is like when God's call strikes into the human heart. It releases a primordial, imposing force that asserts itself against resistances and manages to flourish in the process.

It is always fascinating to reflect on such occurrences. There are mysterious moments in which a mission from God transforms an entire life. This is as true of vocations today as it was in the passages of the Bible that narrate such events. It is the purpose of our book to make the wealth of these ancient stories with their rich experiences and fullness of content accessible to readers of our day.

Our reasons for writing are numerous. Our interest was triggered by encounters and conversations in which we were told about the joy and happiness, but also about the questions and struggles, that people experienced in their vocations. Our book has been written primarily for those who devote themselves entirely to the service of God and other human beings; it is also dedicated to them. We hope that in the light of the biblical texts they will be prompted to understand their own vocations more profoundly and to live them with greater awareness. Perhaps they will also be helped to clarify their decision.

At the same time, however, other men and women may discover that many of the traits found in the vocations described here are to be found in their own lives as well. Those who live their faith with commitment, remain faithful to their mission, and devote themselves selflessly to others share, in their own way, in these special vocations and will see many resemblances.

For both of us, other roots of this book are decades of discipleship as members of the Society of Jesus, a long-term preoccupation with the Bible, and the friendship that unites us.

"At your word" describes the experience that unites all vocations. Just as God's initiative laid hold of great biblical personages such as Moses, Isaiah, Peter, and Paul, so it lays hold of many human beings even today. God forms them into a great community of persons who labor together with complete dedication on the building of his kingdom. They are transformed by the power that comes from their being called by God and that is able to heal the "self" of each of us from destructive and self-centered endeavors.

Crossroads are places where life comes together from various directions and is compressed, as it were. Vocations are such crossing points. They are the points of intersection at which there is a meeting and confrontation between the self-communicating, helping God and human beings who are ready and open; between a previous, usually burdensome history and the new plans of God that aim at salvation; between the special tasks of individuals and the often slow, wait-and-see reactions of communities. As at crossroads in our world, so in the biblical stories of vocations there is an inherent condensing and shifting of life. We invite you to join us in meditating on some decisive moments in which, by means of their "Yes," persons who were called set radically new courses for humanity's history of faith.

The texts presented here are like whole-grain bread that demands a strong bite. The interpretation is based on scholarship, even though it operates on the biblical text as we have it and without footnotes. We have tried not to soften the biblical message, but to let it emerge in its power and individuality. In many cases we have given our own translation based on the wording of the original. The presentation is condensed and demands that readers *read* the relevant biblical text *in advance and keep it open before them.* In this way the divine word can bear better fruit. Since the first chapter in this book (on Ex 3:1—4:17) is exceptionally long due to the explanation of basic matters and makes difficult reading, many readers may prefer to begin with the subsequent call stories.

We have organized all the expositions of the texts on the same pattern. *Situation* provides the historical location of the story in question or, as the case may be, its preceding context. *Structure* briefly addresses the organization of the passage or the literary forms that are used. This is followed by *Interpretation,* which is the main focus of our exposition and usually explains the important elements, verse by verse. Finally, *Perspectives* picks up essential aspects of the interpretation, touches on the subsequent life of those called, and attempts an actualization in the light of contemporary experiences. The concluding *Questions for Reflection* are meant as stimuli for thinking about, or applying to one's own *situation,* what has been observed in the biblical text.

"At your word" also describes the origin of this book, which owes much to the encouragement and help of others. We must mention especially our two religious confreres, Severin Leitner, S.J., and Andreas Batlogg, S.J., as well as the publisher's reader, Thomas Böhm. Their criticisms, suggestions, and formulations have made an important contribution to this work. To them, our special thanks. Finally, we wish to express our gratitude and esteem to Matthew J. O'Connell for his excellent English translation.

Innsbruck   *Georg Fischer, S.J.*
Presentation of the Lord, 1995   *Martin Hasitschka, S.J.*

1

The Burning Bush
God and the Resistance of Moses

Exodus 3:1—4:17

*T*he call of Moses in Exodus 3—4 brings the boldest dreams of humankind to fulfillment. God alone can do humanity the favor of showing himself, making known his name (that is, his inmost being), and stooping to human beings; and that is what he does here for the first time. God's manifestation is not, however, a narcissistic self-portrayal. It is wholly directed to the liberation of dependent and oppressed persons whom God accepts as his own people—a liberation that is the undying hope of those who live exploited and in bondage. The meeting point of all these expectations is the call of Moses, for his mission brings together the longing of humanity, divine power, and an individual's readiness to become the fire that has begun to transform the world ceaselessly with its warmth and light.

Situation

When Moses is called by God in Exodus 3, he is in several ways no longer a *tabula rasa*. We know a great deal from the first two chapters of Exodus about his earlier history and the history of his people. Exodus 1 paints a picture of increasing oppression— forced labor (vv. 9–14); the order to kill newborn boys (vv. 15–21)—of the Israelites, who are visitors, "immigrant workers" in Egypt, a foreign land to them. The text refers to approximately the thirteenth century B.C. The distress of a group or a people is often fertile ground for vocations.

Moses is born into this hostile world. His courageous mother, aided by his sister, saves his life by trickery. Moses owes his life to the courage and competence of these two women as well as to that of a foreign woman, the daughter of the pharaoh, who disobeys the command of her own father out of pity (2:1–10 with 1:22). With compassionate courage these women fight for the little child. Their loving care is the bud from which the deliverance of the people will later blossom. Moses is able to grow up in the shelter of his family and amid the traditions of his people and his faith. In addition, he receives an education at pharaoh's highly civilized court with its many cosmopolitan connections. Against all expectations, crisis and hostility become a blessing for Moses: he receives a superior, indeed a twofold, education.

Where does Moses stand now? Has the luxury of the court softened him and turned him into an Egyptian? Exodus 2:11 and following answers this question. Three scenes in a row show the strong acting unjustly toward the underdog. On each occasion Moses stands up for the weak. In the process he becomes a murderer himself (2:12). The isolation into which he is now thrust by his own actions is made clear to him by the question of a fellow countryman: "Who made you a ruler and judge over us?" (2:14). Although he knows the risks he takes in standing up for others and must flee as a result, he does not change his attitude. Instead, in alien Midian, where he has no rights and no protection, he resists, though alone, some shepherds who outnumber him; and he helps some unknown women exercise their rights (2:17). This unbridled, untamable longing for justice shapes the character of Moses.

Therefore, when God calls this Moses for his mission in Exodus 3, he chooses a man who has already been molded in many respects. Moses is familiar with two cultures: the culture formed by the traditional faith of his people and the modern, progressive, splendid world of the Egyptian court. His later mission will require an openness to and an understanding of both of these worlds. It seems to be characteristic of God's missions that they take place in such border zones between two cultures or positions:

for Moses it was Egypt and Israel; for Elijah and Hosea, the worship of Baal and the worship of Yahweh; for Jesus, a religion hardened in place and the call to conversion; in our day it is secular prosperity and Christian faith. Being profoundly familiar with both and yet being entirely on God's side—this is what makes a mission fruitful.

But in calling Moses, God is also calling a man who has incurred heavy guilt and has lived for many years with this guilt and borne its consequences. Yet in God's eyes his burdened past and great guilt are not an obstacle to his being called. God gives the persecuted and isolated Moses a new chance. Jesus too calls sinners to follow him (Levi in Mk 2:13ff.; Peter in Lk 5:8). Today, sinful men and women still can receive God's call. Their guilt is not an obstacle to their vocation.

Finally, Moses is deeply motivated by his longing for justice (see Mt 5:6); he devotes himself untiringly to it, even when it cuts him off from his own and forces him to flee abroad. God can use men whose hearts are thus on fire.

We may get the impression that until Exodus 2:22 God has hardly been present to the Israelites in their distress. Apart from his support for the midwives Shiphrah and Puah (Ex 1:15–20), he is not mentioned. There are times when people ask why God does not intervene against injustice, violence, and oppression. The long wait of the Israelites for deliverance is matched by the experience of many people today: God has seemingly withdrawn and does not care about their suffering. He does not intervene. He allows wickedness to spread, despite its emptiness, until people collapse under it; and he allows goodness to suffer and grow under such conditions. But suddenly, in Exodus 2:23–25, the situation changes. God becomes profoundly aware of the desperate plight of the Israelites in Egypt (God and verbs of perception occur five times in the passage), and he responds by coming and appointing Moses. The sending of those he calls is God's answer to the distress of human beings.

Exodus 3:1—4:17 describes the first call given in the Bible. It has characteristic, basic features. In the Old Testament a "call" is expressed not by the verb *call,* but by the two verbs *send* and *go* (3:10ff.), as well as by the use of a set series of elements or "call pattern" (see below under Structure). The use of these verbs already shows that in the Hebrew text it is not so much the aspect of calling (and thus of some audible speech from God) that is emphasized, but the aspect of acceptance of a task ("sending") and its implementation ("go"). In the Old Testament, people thus called are "messengers of God" who go forth on his account to carry out his orders. It is not some spectacular, extraordinary event but the execution of a divine commission that is the heart of a vocation. It would be a mistake for us today to expect, for example, an audible call or a visible manifestation as confirmation of a vocation.

Exodus 3:1—4:17 is the first and, apart from Ezekiel 1—3, also the lengthiest call in the Old Testament. When the text was written down (probably in the sixth century B.C., or even later), the writer, looking back from centuries of experience of God and his messengers, incorporated into the call of Moses certain essential, fundamental characteristics of such calls. Exodus 3:1—4:17 depicts, with a fullness not found elsewhere, the decisive traits of such an event, both on the side of God who sends and of the human being who goes on behalf of God.

Structure

The reader of Exodus 3:1—4:17 has the impression of being faced with a text that advances clearly and smoothly and is easily understood. This is the result of a careful structuring that respects several points of view and is still recognizable today.

The semantic fields alone give rise to two principles for dividing the passage. The dominant verbs are: *see* (3:1–9), *go* and *send* (3:10–22), *believe* and *listen* [to the voice] (4:1–9), and *speak* (4:10–17). These key verbs divide our text into four sections, but at the same time an inner connecting line and a tension run through these. There is a movement from "seeing"—the meeting of the two parties and the perception of the distress—to "sending." This movement elicits "believing/listening" from the one addressed. But this is possible only through the "speaking" that communicates the divine message. In regard to the divine call, this means that sending results from the encounter with God and is directed toward the belief of a community. In the process, speaking—that is, the ability to communicate—plays a decisive role.

While the verbs thus account for the dynamic aspect of the passage, a series of distinctive features registers the static aspect. A special vocabulary, which is used exclusively or predominantly in particular sections and often repeated in successive verses, makes it possible, when combined with "ending markers" (repetitions coming at the end), to divide Exodus 3:1—4:17 into six pictures:

3:1–6.   The setting of the scene, marked by, among other things, *"bush," "turn aside," "fire," "burn."*

3:7–12.   God's request, with *"Egypt"* recurring in each verse. From v. 9 on, Egypt is contrasted with *"Israelites,"* and from v. 10 on, with *"bring out."*

3:13–15.   The sender and the *"Name."* Mention is still made of the Israelites; discourse in the second person plural begins.

3:16–22.   Yahweh's plan; *"Egypt,"* from the second picture, recurs again, as does *"you"* in the plural from the third picture.

4:1–9.   Confirming signs: *"hand," "snake," "cloak," "sign."*

4:10–17.   Mission extended to Aaron: *"mouth," "slow of tongue," "teach."*

Notice that the last two pictures are coextensive with the sections of Exodus 4 that are marked by believing/hearing and speaking, respectively, while the first four pictures subdivide

Exodus 3 more precisely and in a different way. We can regard these six pictures as successive "takes" on a single event; they set before us in a clear-cut way, with appropriate vocabulary, essential phases of this event. This kind of subdivision of a lengthy text is necessary and helpful for grasping its important themes (see Interpretation below).

From the viewpoint of acting and speaking, our passage shows a clear division. An abundance of actions and outward incidents occur almost solely at the beginning, in Exodus 3:1–6. From 3:7 on and to the end in 4:17, apart from a few short remarks (4:3f., 6f., and 14), the call of Moses consists exclusively of dialogue, introduced at each step by the typical Hebrew introduction to a statement, "And he said." The phrase is used eight times of Moses, but fifteen times of God, which means that God speaks approximately twice as often as Moses, and if we look at the length of his speeches (the number of words), even five times more than Moses. Altogether then, God plays the leading part in the conversation: he begins it (3:4), carries it on, and ends it (4:14–17). The high proportion of speech in our text points to something of exceptional importance, which the narrator communicates in an unadulterated way and, so to speak, in the "original tone" of the direct speech between the affected persons (God and Moses).

The high number of outward incidents has drawn our attention to the difference between Exodus 3:1–6 and the following verses. These first six verses are in fact comparable to what is called "setting the scene" in a play: the personages, the place, the time, and other essential circumstances of the action are introduced. The hearers/readers of the story have the information they need for becoming familiar with the situation, and this they must do. Along with Moses, we find ourselves on holy ground near the burning bush on the mountain of God, and we hear the voice of God. This scene is meant to remain as a picture before our eyes throughout the entire text.

The setting of the scene corresponds to what Ignatius of Loyola calls the "composition of place" in meditative prayer. Biblical narratives, including stories of calls, usually give the relevant data about the situation at the beginning, as is the case here. It is worth our while to take seriously the symbolism of these often skimpy, seemingly peripheral details, for they anticipate essential elements in a symbolic and often compressed form.

In addition to what has been said thus far, it must be noted that Exodus 3:1—4:17 follows two further patterns. The first is a form that occurs in other biblical stories and has been described as the "call pattern" (W. Richter). In a number of passages we meet the following five elements, often in the same order (at the end of each, New Testament parallels are given in parentheses):

Reference to distress, 3:7, 9: A situation of injustice or suffering leads to God's intervention (see Mt 9:35–38: Jesus' pity on the people, who are like "sheep without a shepherd").

Commission, 3:10: The key words are *send* and *go;* in response to a human distress, God lays on an individual a charge that can demand a great deal of him, to the point even of a radical change in way of life (see Mt 10:5f.: the sending of the Twelve as Jesus' response to the people being "sheep without a shepherd").

Objection, 3:11: The person addressed believes that he is unworthy, unsuitable, or incapable for some reason. With his objection he resists the divine mission. This element brings out more strongly the human side or view of the call (see Lk 9:58f., 61: the objections of those whom Jesus calls; see also Peter in Lk 5:8).

Assurance, 3:12: The classical formula is "I will be with you." This promise of assistance assures the commissioned person that he need not go alone, that God remains involved with him in his mission (see Jesus' promise of assistance in Mt

28:20; in a reversal of the formula, the first task of the Twelve is to be with Jesus: Mk 3:14).

Sign, 3:12: An outward event or material sign confirms the divine nature of the mission (see the deeds done by the disciples, Mk 16:17f.; see also the commissioning speeches in Mt 10:8 and Mk 6:7, 13).

These five elements occur in almost the same sequence in, for example, Judges 6, Jeremiah 1, and in part or with deviations in almost all the Old Testament passages discussed in this book. Thus we are in the presence of a model or type that clearly displays in its essential traits a consistent structure, a model that recurs even today. If God sends persons in the present age, he does so in answer to some distress. When those whom he calls raise objections and have difficulties, this reflects not some malice or rejection on their part, but links them in solidarity with such great figures as Moses, Isaiah, and Jeremiah. That God does not abandon those whom he calls is confirmed by the final two elements: his presence and power accompany those who risk their lives for his mission.

The peculiarity of Exodus 3:1—4:17 is that many elements of this call pattern occur not just once but several times. Thus assurances are given again in 4:12 and 15. However, the element repeated most often is the objection. Exodus 3:1—4:17 tells five times (a frequency not found elsewhere in the Old Testament) of Moses' resistance to the mission.

A second pattern found in this passage is called "account of the sending of the liberator." This pattern includes as many as seventeen elements. It is also to be found in other ancient Near Eastern texts. From this pattern common to Exodus 3:1—4:17 and other stories, it can be inferred that Moses is here being sent as a "liberator," a rescuer, and that he will be successful. In God's commission to him we do not have the appointment of, for example, a prophet; but we have the sending of a human being who will set his people free.

Interpretation

Setting the Scene (Ex 3:1–6)

Right at the beginning, Moses is presented in his everyday work as a shepherd in the service of, and dependent on, his father-in-law. This occupation is typical of his people (see Gn 47:3); in it he learns responsibility, far-sightedness, caring, and obedience. In these ways he is practicing for his future task of leading his people (like David, see 1 Sm 16). His customary activity is thus a preparation, and it is during this period that God calls him. Nowadays, vocations often mature in a similar manner in the everyday life of a student or a professional, and the experiences of that time leave their mark on the future activity.

The indications of place at the end of verse 1 deserve attention. "Beyond the wilderness" is a phrase that occurs only here in the Bible. It may be a hint that this Moses pushes things to the limit, dares novelty. He is one who in the routine of everyday life has kept a sense of the unusual and who is also gifted with it, as shown in this case by his coming to the mountain of God. Both "wilderness" and "mountain" have symbolic meanings. "Wilderness" is the place where human beings cannot live on their own, where they come up against the limitations of their existence. "Mountain," as a connection between heaven and earth, is the privileged place of encounter with God. Thus viewed, wilderness and mountain are also symbols of the spiritual way of people today. Even in the wilderness of an often materialistic, unbelieving society there are mountains on which God's goodness and greatness are experienced.

In this setting God makes himself known first of all in the figure of his messenger ("angel," v. 2), who manifests himself as a flame in a bush. Rabbinical exegesis and the fathers of the church have seen in God's coming in this bush an image of his descent into human lowliness. God makes himself known, not in a great towering tree, but in a little plant, in solidarity with the suffering of those being oppressed in Egypt.

God's way of showing himself is a paradoxical one. On the one hand, there is fire: a sign of the divine presence (e.g., Ex 19:18) and a consuming, destructive force. On the other hand, this fire does not burn up the bush. The picture suggests a divine power that does not annihilate but seeks to transform things interiorly. Isaiah 43:2 offers this experience as a promise for distressed believers. This paradoxical aspect of God's self-communication also leaves its mark on the text that follows (for example, the signs of the staff/snake, the healthy/leprous hand, water/blood in 4:1–19 and elsewhere) and is a characteristic of biblical speech about God that has received little attention. Yahweh is the one who knows how to combine experiences that are contradictory from the human point of view. Whereas human beings often hold blindly to a position with the result that they come in conflict with others and foster enmities, God in his expansiveness embraces seeming opposites.

Moses is not satisfied with merely observing this strange phenomenon. In the wilderness, where every extra effort brings increased difficulty and, depending on circumstances, can even be dangerous, he makes a detour ("turn aside," v. 3). Even after great disappointments and after long years in a foreign land and after forming his own family (Ex 2), he remains alert and interested. Resignation or comfort have not conquered him. I am reminded of an unforgettable colleague who, though over ninety, followed all the important events in the world and the church with openness and attention.

As Moses makes his way to the bush, God calls him: "Moses! Moses!" (v. 4). A call with repetition of the name occurs only four times in the Old Testament (Gn 22:11; 46:2; here; and 1 Sm 3:10) and three times in the New Testament (Lk 10:41; 22:31; Acts 9:4). On each occasion it represents a high point or turning point for the one addressed. The naming of the name makes the call personal; the doubling of the name makes it urgent. Those so addressed are earnestly challenged by God in their inmost identity. God does not call robots; he calls persons by their names, in their individuality and capacity for relationships, and in virtue of his intimate closeness to them.

Moses does not yet know who is speaking to him. All the more surprising to him, then, are the demands in verse 5, which impose on him distance and subordination (symbolized by the removal of his sandals). To wear sandals is the prerogative of free persons (Ex 12:11; Lk 15:22), whereas servants and prisoners had to go barefoot (e.g., Is 20:2). Sandals also serve as a sign of power or legal entitlement; to enter a region while wearing them can mean that the wearer has a claim to that region (Is 11:15; Ps 60:10; and, in connection with levirate marriage, Dt 25:9f.; Ru 4:7f.). When Moses here removes his sandals (this is not reported but is taken for granted), he acknowledges that he is standing on foreign ("holy") ground and is no longer his own master. He thus surrenders his self-determination, so to speak. A call is often the beginning and exercise of an ever greater surrender of one's self.

Only in verse 6 does God reveal his identity to Moses. His description of himself is marked by relationships: to "your" (Moses') father and to the three patriarchs, who are named here as a series for the third time (after Gn 50:24 and Ex 2:24) and for the first time in connection with God. In Judaism this is interpreted as fidelity through three generations and therefore as permanent. But even before this, God speaks of his connection with the faith practiced in the family of Moses ("the God of your father"). This God is not a stranger.

Nevertheless, Moses is fearful and hides his face from this God. His fear is probably connected with the basic principle enunciated in Exodus 33:20 (see also Jgs 13:22 and Is 6:5) that human beings cannot endure a direct encounter with God (seeing his "face"). According to a conception common in the Old Testament, God's essence and sovereignty are so far above everything human that direct contact with them brings death. Now, at the end of this opening scene before the burning bush, Moses, who went up to see, no longer sees because his face is hidden.

In this setting of the scene we find a very rich set of symbols: wilderness, mountain, bush, fire, removal of sandals, hiding one's face, and so on. Exodus 3:1–6 contains, in a highly concentrated form, a wealth of elements that usually occur only singly in other stories of calls or of divine manifestations. This wealth is in keeping with the special importance of both the event and the text.

At the same time, the first six verses supply portraits of the two chief personages. Confronting each other are a God who takes the initiative and is interested in Moses, and Moses, a fascinating human being. In paradoxical fashion God combines supreme power with mercy and with coming in lowly form. Moses has not allowed himself to be discouraged by the blows of fate or to be limited in his alertness and readiness by things that make his life secure (family, occupation). On the contrary, despite circumstances that make things more difficult (wilderness, not knowing who is addressing him) he lets himself in for something new. Even when in the presence of God he loses his freedom of movement, his self-determination ("sandals"), his initiative, and even his sight ("hiding his face"), he responds to everything.

There is often confusion at the beginning of a vocation. The old familiar world does not hold together any longer; the high motives and good attitudes that previously gave verve and strength in deciding on a spiritual path collide with a completely altered field of action: a different way of life, coexistence in a community with people previously unknown, new tasks or even no tasks. Much that previously went to make up the "I" with all its strengths has suddenly disappeared. The question inevitably arises: "Am I on the right path? I was determined to put myself generously at God's disposal, and now I find that I am able to do increasingly less, that many of my abilities are being restricted." At the beginning this feeling of diminishment can confuse those who are called. In this situation it can help to look at Moses and see in this "relegation" a necessary step and a provisional phase. The temporary lack of freedom, the blindness, and the immobilization that Moses experiences are the prelude to his leading an entire people to freedom and to God and to his own attainment of the highest vision of God (Ex 34:6–7, 29ff.).

God's Request (Ex 3:7–12)

Three verbs in verse 7 (see, hear, know) and their form (*see* is strengthened by the absolute infinitive) underscore the fact that God is deeply aware of the distress described in Exodus 1 and 2. In God's words, the expression "my people" occurs for the first time in the Bible. God says of a group of dirty, unjustly treated "foreign workers" that they are his people. God is here entering into solidarity with people being oppressed in a foreign land, or to put it realistically, with a tattered mob of human beings.

God does not simply express his awareness; he has already intervened to rescue ("I have come down," v. 8). The goal of this liberation is a beautiful, almost paradisal land, overflowing with the best foods and capable of supporting six nations.

While it has not been said thus far in the dialogue just who this people of God is, verse 9 specifies them as "children of Israel/Israelites." The beginning of the book of Exodus marks the transition in which this designation of the descendants of the patriarch Jacob/Israel becomes a designation for a people. Verses 9 and 10 are linked together by the introductory "and now," with verse 9 harking back by way of explanation to God's awareness as described in verse 7, and with verse 10 expressing the consequence of that awareness.

As in the broader context (Ex 1f. with 3f.), so in the narrower, it becomes clear that the sending of a human being is God's answer to a present distress. God's intervention in order to liberate (v. 8) seeks here to gain support and collaboration: the commission given to Moses, his mission, is, as it were, the reverse side of the divine intervention. The honor bestowed on all who are called is that they are to collaborate with God. His and their work are one and the same.

Moses responds, not enthusiastically, but with a question (v. 11), which, except for the words *send* and *people,* repeats God's commission verbatim. The introductory "Who am I?" (as in 1 Sm 18:18 and 2 Sm 7:18) is meant to suggest his own unworthiness and is an expression of humility. On a deeper level, however, this first objection of Moses signals the fact that the "I," the person of the one called, is decisive in every mission. As long as the question "Who am I?" is unsettled or not at least asked, the mission to and identification with the target group are also problematic (note the two words omitted in Moses' objection). The "I" accompanies the one called as a loyal companion his whole life through, both in success and in conflicts. This requires that he remain vigilant regarding his own person and that he be constantly aware of his own strengths and weaknesses. Every call is closely and inseparably connected with the person of the one called.

God rallies Moses with a promise and a sign (v. 12), but the kind of sign given is unique. A sign usually relates to the present; the one receiving is able to grasp its divine character immediately. But the sign given to Moses is announced as something future. The worship of God on Mount Sinai by the entire people is then the fulfillment both of the sign and of the mission itself in the highest degree: an encounter with God in freedom as experienced by the entire community. This sign surpasses all external, material signs, which depend on faith and often do not find it (Nm 14:11; Mt 12:38ff.; Jn 12:37). There are few things that can support and sustain those called as much as a journeying together in faith. Many church workers experience their activity in communities as a gift: they derive courage from the deep and heartfelt trust in God of many people. To live, pray, and sing together with others binds people together as a community and with God.

Exodus 3:7–12 shows us what it is that concerns God. Deeply compassionate, God is not indifferent to the situation of poor, oppressed foreigners. He intends to deliver them from the enslaving power that is here given the symbolic name of "Egypt," which stands in principle for every exercise of power that is inhuman and opposed to God. In this deliverance God wants to use human collaboration. But he does not simply claim this help; he also heeds the difficulties (objections) of those he calls and responds to them.

The Name of the Sender (Ex 3:13–15)

Most call stories end with a promise and a sign. In the case of Moses, however, further objections, along with God's answers, are reported. As a result, light is shed on the call process to a degree not found elsewhere. Paradoxically, it is precisely the multiplied objections of Moses, the expression of his resistance, that lead to a multiplication of God's promises. God confirms the mission of Moses as he does no other.

The second objection (v. 13) has to do with the person of the sender, the "thou" of God. It is significant that the use of the second person singular in addressing God is missing precisely here in this context. Instead, Moses makes masterful use of a hypothetical future case, which introduces, with "suppose," three conditions, and ends with two questions. Speaking of God in the third person helps Moses avoid the more familiar "thou."

The hypothetical acceptance of the mission ("if/suppose I come") leads to helplessness ("What shall I say to them?"). Meanwhile, however, Moses gracefully introduces a very brief dialogue in which the words "God of your fathers" casts a significant light on him. If he followed God's self-description in verse 6, he should have said "God of our fathers." The use of the second person plural "your" shows Moses keeping a distance similar to that in verse 11, where he did not use the expression "my people" from verse 10.

The questioning response of the Israelites is to be viewed on several levels. To begin with, Moses formulates it in his objection (a). Then the question itself has two meanings: What is his name?/What does his name mean? The "name" stands for the essence, the person of God. To know the meaning of this name (b) and the name of God (c) are of decisive importance for the one sent and also for legitimizing him to the people to whom he is sent.

In verses 14–15 God answers at all three levels. First of all (level a: v. 14a), Moses hears: "I will be whoever I will be." This communication, which is meant for Moses himself, emphasizes the point that God is not at anyone's disposal. Even though he now makes his name known, the knowledge of this name cannot be misused as a means to power or for magical purposes. The repeated "I will be" implies God's existence in the future and, as a result, certainty in a realm to which human beings do not have access on their own. The peculiar construction of the relative clause (represented by "whoever") emphasizes even further this freedom of God. No human being can decide how God must behave. He remains free throughout the entire future.

God's second answer is meant for the Israelites (level b: v. 14b). With the words "I will be" (Hebrew: *'ehjeh*) it refers back to the first answer, the one to Moses, and says that the God who reveals himself in this way is the source of the mission. At the same time this answer, while increasing the tension, serves as a transition to the solemn unveiling of the divine name *Yahweh* (level c: v. 15), which is phonetically close to *'ehjeh* and appears to be the transposition of *'ehjeh* into the third person ("the Lord" in NRSV = Yahweh = "he will be"). The complete name has five parts (as does that of the Egyptian pharaoh): "Yahweh, the God of your ancestors, the God of Abraham, the God of Isaac, and the God of Jacob." God's further words in verse 15 are, in their form, an account of institution (comparable in its elements to the institution of the Last Supper in 1 Cor 11:23–26) and thereby make it clear that God wants to be forever called by this name.

Behind the talk about God's name during the call lies a fundamental experience: an interior knowledge of God is the supporting basis of every mission. Only those to whom God has manifested his being are able to go forth on his behalf. This experience does not mean that human beings have power over God, but this gift of God's closeness does persist, even in the future over which we have no control, as a firm foundation for those whom he sends. Their familiarity with God, which grows over the years, offers direction and protection to others.

Yahweh's Plan (Ex 3:16–22)

Not only does God gift Moses with his name, but he also tells him about the main stages of the liberation. These lead from the winning of support among the people (v. 16f.) to negotiations with the pharaoh (v. 18), which need to be backed up by divine manifestations of power (v. 19f.), and finally to an amicable parting (v. 21f.). These verses give Moses clear direction and a broad view. What he is told helps him to organize his activity in accordance with God's plan. He is thus able to carry out the difficult and complex plan of liberation.

Moses is instructed to seek the help of others in carrying out his mission. This means, first of all, winning over the elders (v. 16), a group of responsible, influential people who are, after Moses and Aaron, the privileged addressees and witnesses of the divine action in the book of Exodus (Ex 4:29f.; 12:21; 17:5f.; 19:7; 24:1, 9, and other occasions). They are even given an abbreviated summary of Yahweh's revelation to Moses ending in verse 17 with the manifestation of his innermost thoughts (introduced by "And I thought/said"). Thus the confidence of the dying Joseph (Gn 50:24) that God would look after them in Egypt is justified. The road leads from a wretched life in a foreign land to the Promised Land that has already been described in glowing terms in verse 8.

The next stage in God's plan is for Moses and the elders to appear together before the pharaoh with the declaration: "The Lord, the God of the Hebrews, has met with us." Their statement ends with their desire: "that we may sacrifice to the Lord our

God." This is the first occurrence in the Bible of this expression of a common faith: "The Lord our God." God, who appears to Moses, sets human beings free, and in doing so, he also joins them together in unity. Men and women who are called are not solo fighters. They are successful in their task only if they fill others with enthusiasm for God's cause and win them as collaborators. Their joint action then has the power to tackle obstacles and take a public position.

As a rule, such plans meet with the resistance of those, symbolized here by the Egyptian king (v. 19), who profit from the disunity of others and their lack of organization. Tyrants often seem to understand no language but that of force, which God uses as a last resort when all negotiations have failed (v. 20, advance notice of the plagues). Even then, in the end they want to hold on to the exercise of power and even to order the departure: (literally) "the king of Egypt will send you away."

In contrast to this situation is the departure of the people from Egypt in verses 21–22, which takes place as if among friends. Valuable souvenirs ("jewelry of silver and gold") and articles of clothing will be requested and given to the departing Hebrews. The traditional translation of the final clause as "you shall plunder" (and again in 12:36) is not at all appropriate and is all the more puzzling since elsewhere the Hebrew verb always means "rescue, liberate" (e.g., above, in v. 8). The explanatory passages (Ex 11:1–3 and 12:35f.) likewise depict an atmosphere of friendship between Egyptians and Israelites (favor, mercy, good will), for the departure of the latter frees the former from the fear of death (12:33) and thus rescues them.

Although Moses still does not know all the details of his task, he has received a general idea of it that guides his movements. This kind of knowledge of basic direction and essential stages will help him make distinctions and decisions regarding his mission. An essential element in this knowledge is that while God's role is, if need be, to respond to violent resistance with violence, the tasks of those he sends are to unite the people in faith and to represent this unity before others. In this whole process, it is in God's interest that there be peaceful relations between the peoples (v. 21f.). Even though their interests differ, those whom God calls should work for an amicable mutual understanding for the good of all.

Confirming Signs (Ex 4:1–9)

In Moses' third objection (4:1) the beneficiaries of the mission, "they," come on the scene alongside the "I" of the one sent and the "You/He" of God the sender. In his objection, Moses harks back to what God says in 3:16 and 18, and denies it in an uncompleted conditional sentence that once again (as in 3:13) shows him to be at a loss and set apart from his own people. Unlike God, he counts on the Israelites being incredulous. In this he expresses the experience that many called by God have had down to our own time, namely, that their mission is often not accepted and meets with resistance. He also shows how those called initially think and argue out of anxiety that their message may not be accepted, and this even before they have come in touch with the addressees of what they have to say.

God answers Moses by giving three signs that, step by step, suggest power over three different realms. The change of a staff into a snake and back again (v. 3f.) represents the realm of things and wild animals, the inanimate and the animate; the change in the hand to leprous and its reversal (v. 6f.) represents the entire realm of health and community (to be a leper led to exclusion from the community: Lv 13:45f.); and the change of water into blood (v. 9) represents in principle life and death. The man being commissioned is made subject to these elemental powers: Moses experiences the threat to his life ("draw back," at the end of v. 3), the overcoming of his fear (grasping the snake, v. 4), and menacing sickness (leprosy, v. 6) in his own body. Personal familiarity with such boundary experiences is a preparation for mission. It helps the one sent to understand others in their suffering and to be close to them.

Here, however, everything has yet another function. As signs of divine power (recall here their paradoxical character, which is expressed in 3:2 as well), they also lend the one sent authority in the eyes of the people. By his unexpected and surprising explanations (discourse without introduction in v. 5 and 8f.), God connects the signs closely with the "faith" that follows upon them. That is, this faith is directed to the message communicated by Moses ("that the Lord has appeared to you," v. 5; compare v. 1 with 3:16), to the messenger himself ("you," v. 8), to the "voice" (content, meaning) of the sign (v. 8), and even to the sign itself (v. 9). In this context, then, "faith" means the knowledge gained in connection with the sign and the acceptance of the divine origin of the mission. Even if someone tried to evade this powerful legitimation, the "blood on the dry ground" (v. 9; see Gn 4:10, "from the ground") would bring him to the edge of death. Anyone not believing God's messenger and his message despite all these manifestations of power is risking his life.

God's envoys do not go unprotected and helpless. They bring with them signs that show them to be holders of divine power. In our day it is necessary to distinguish here between a false emphasis on "signs" (apparitions, private revelations, demands for healing, great public spectacles, and so on) that call for caution in acceptance and, at the other extreme, a rationalistic reserve that restricts faith to the private realm and in so doing often reduces it solely to the level of thought. A mission from God, on the other hand, has an innate power that those called and those around them experience in very concrete ways from its effects in everyday life. Here the world becomes a place of love, understanding, community, self-surrender. The experience of brotherhood and sisterhood is the mightiest sign for human beings and, at the same time, a witness to the triune, loving God.

Extension of the Mission to Aaron (Ex 4:10–17)

After the questions (the uncompleted conditional sentence in 4:1 can also be regarded as a question) asked by way of objection have so far proved fruitless, Moses resorts to entreaties ("O my Lord," v. 10). His humble admission of his complete incompetence ("never, in the past, now, slow of speech, slow of tongue") is intended to convince God that he has chosen an unsuitable human being.

Many critics have suspected a speech defect of some kind as the basis for this negative self-description of Moses as one unable to speak. But a careful study of his speech, both here and in the rest of the book of Exodus, shows that he was a dazzling orator. While the first three objections are already brilliant linguistic gems, 4:10, with its two expressions that are unique in the Bible ("eloquent" = literally, "man of words"; and "slow of speech"), with its balanced, three-part formula for time and its humble self-description, is a little literary masterpiece. Moses' claim to be unable to speak is a linguistically convincing proof of his outstanding eloquence.

How is this resistance to be interpreted? The difference between the content (inability to speak) and form (elegant speech) reflects the discrepancy, often observable in those called, between their subjective evaluation of themselves and their objective ability. While those around them rejoice at their intervention and proclamation and are satisfied with it, and while this feeling corresponds to the reality, many of those called judge their own abilities to be unsatisfactory and inadequate.

The resistance also illustrates a constant experience of pastoral life, one that comes to the surface most keenly in connection with weekly sermons: it is beyond the power of human beings to transmit God's word in an effective and attractive way. Those called to preach have been given a commission that brings them up against their own limitations and demands that they go beyond these.

In this setting God's answer to Moses in verse 11 turns the latter's gaze away from his anxious focus on himself to the breadth of God's creative power. By his reference to the gifts and obstacles that originate in him, God liberates Moses from the ever narrowing circles of the hopeless spiral into which he is forced by his dissatisfaction with his own achievements or gifts and his search for recognition, even in his mission. Moses must be satisfied with the fact that Yahweh has made every human being, and therefore Moses as well, to be what he is. The acceptance of this creaturehood is our first mission, and precisely therein the handicapped often far outstrip the healthy in their willingness and freedom.

God's increasing impatience with Moses breaks out in the repeated demand, "Now go!" (3:10, 16, and now 4:12). He expects Moses now to act, and to this end he gives him a special promise ("I will be with your mouth") that will make up for his supposed weakness as a speaker, together with a further promise to be Moses' teacher. One who has God as teacher can tackle anything.

But Moses is still unable to agree: "O my Lord, please send someone else" (v. 13). Courteously, and in the form of a plea, Moses makes it clear that he is unwilling and that God had better look around for someone else. This last objection is an open refusal of the mission. Nothing of this kind is reported anywhere else in the Bible in verbal form, though it does occur in the form of action in Jonah's flight. Moses cannot even give reasons for his decision. But if we look at the decision in the context of the entire dialogue we see that we have reached the very heart of his resistance to the mission. After the roles of everyone concerned (objections 1–3: Moses, God, the people) and Moses' own suitability ("speaking," 4:10) have been addressed, the issue here is the will and feelings of Moses. An interior uneasiness causes Moses to say no to God, even though (beginning with the fourth objection) he has now reached a direct relationship with God, as we see from the way he uses familiar address.

Often it is only a good, open, personal relationship that makes it possible for those called to express their deepest feelings.

It is crucial that those called honestly see their own misgivings with utmost clarity and express them to God. The concealment or covering up of objections or obstacles does not do away with them. The expression of them is a sign of trust in God and finds him to be supportive, even five times over as is the case here.

In light of all God's efforts thus far, his annoyance ("anger," v. 14) is understandable, although it finds surprisingly mild expression in the question about Aaron. Descent, fluency in speaking, and closeness to Moses make Aaron well suited for taking over the mission along with his brother. Verses 16–17 regulate the division of roles between the two. It is for Moses to communicate God's words to his brother, and for Aaron to pass them on to the people. The precedence of Moses over Aaron is expressed by the status name "God," in whose place Moses stands in relation to Aaron (in Ex 7:1 in relation to the pharaoh). The promises of special assistance in speaking and teaching (v. 12) are repeated for both men. The words *staff* and *signs* in the concluding verse 17 hark back to the fifth image; by telling Moses to take the staff, God points out the first concrete step and so helps Moses to tackle his mission.

The last scene brings a stirring emotional finale. The fourth objection in 4:10 picks up the "hearing/believing" of the addressees, but goes into the complementary side of that hearing, namely, the speaking (ability to speak) of the one called. Thus it returns to the person of Moses and specifically to his aptitude (capabilities) and inclination (his unwillingness in the final objection, 4:13).

In face of Moses' supposed inability and his unexplained unwillingness, God remains unmoved. He increases his promises, turns the focus from the "I" of the one called to broader contexts, and facilitates the acceptance of the mission by the inclusion in it of a brother. Yahweh thus shows himself to be one who has sympathy for the difficulties of Moses, takes them seriously, and helps him in a concrete way to overcome them.

The commissioning of the brother certainly plays a decisive role in this process. It is a major support to have someone else, a close friend, at one's side in the mission. Furthermore, this kind of partnership makes it much easier to ensure that God and his message will be central and that the person of those called will not be thrust into the foreground. Even so, those called retain their lofty distinction: They represent God and embody him.

Perspectives

The longest dialogue in the Bible between God and a human being sparkles like a diamond. It owes its radiance to the five objections of Moses, since they broaden the conversation and move it along. In what he says, Moses reveals himself and comes ever closer to the heart of his interior resistance, while at the same time he comes to a more direct and honest relationship with God. In the process Yahweh, for his part, displays countless radiant facets of himself: he adapts himself to Moses with understanding and patience, communicates himself with a hitherto unknown openness, enters into solidarity with people suffering in a foreign land, and intends to liberate human beings and unite them in a community of faith. With the mission of Moses God also commits himself. He takes over the responsibility for his envoys and for his plan to rescue "Israel," which is the symbolic name for all who believe in him.

While the objections raised in the dialogue may give the impression that Moses struggles by every possible means against his mission, the immediate continuation in 4:18–19 makes it clear that he now follows God's orders freely and with inner conviction (the key word "go" occurs three times in the Hebrew text; it translates as "go back" and "went back"). The voluntary acceptance of the mission here in 4:18 throws light on God's behavior of just a moment ago. His answer to Moses' refusal in 4:13 could have been interpreted as coercion, inasmuch as he does not agree with Moses' wish. But in the additional sending of Aaron, God shows that he has accurately gotten at what is really motivating Moses, something that Moses himself is yet unable to express and that represents the last major difficulty in the way of the mission: the demand that he take up such a commission by himself is an excessive one, from which everyone naturally shrinks. God sympathetically accommodates himself to Moses by sending Aaron as well. Today, too, every call has the support of brothers and sisters. The ever new individuals to whom God speaks enter into the vast, unceasing community of those who through the ages have put themselves at God's disposal in a special way. They are not alone.

Linked with Moses' obedience in 4:18 is his concern for his "brothers/kindred" in Egypt. In contrast to the threefold distancing of himself from them during the dialogue ("my people" is missing in 3:11; "God of your fathers," 3:13; "Suppose they do not believe me," 4:1), Moses here feels that he is in solidarity with his oppressed fellow Hebrews and identifies himself with them. The information from 2:23 that is repeated in 4:19, namely, that those who were hunting for him have died, opens the way for Moses to return. Moses did not even mention this risk in the dialogue. The danger to his life if he accepted the mission was evidently something he took for granted, or else he regarded the other objections he raised as more weighty. There have always been a great number of persons called who have paid for their commitment with persecution, imprisonment, or even their lives. Such recent heroes as Dietrich Bonhoeffer, Alfred Delp, S.J., Archbishop Oscar Romero, and many others, including persons unknown, bear witness to this fact.

Moses too is not spared such clashes. After initial success (Ex 4:27–37), his course leads him into ever more serious conflicts. Reproaches from his own people (5:21), the ceaseless maneuvering and stalling of the pharaoh to the point even of threatening Moses with death (10:38), the mockery of his fellow countrymen and their claim to superior insight in the face of human hopelessness (14:11)—these are part of his mission. Just as in the call of Moses God answered the question of the source of Moses' authority (2:14), so in all these conflicts (and those later on in the wilderness) he gives his promised assistance to Moses and supports him in everything. The only exception is the threat in 4:24–26, but this is to be understood as a "rite of transition." Since Moses has survived this supreme divine threat (resulting perhaps from his own act of slaying in 2:12 or from God's anger in 4:14) with the help of his family and of the rites of his faith, there is nothing more that can now check his mission. Moses can rely completely on God and will thereby, along with God, become himself a support for his people (14:31).

Moses is the ideal of a person called in the Old Testament. In the fire of the encounter with God he is profoundly transformed, becoming like the one for whom he goes. The final description of him as "God" in 4:16 confirms this close link. He who at one time had great plans and who established his family in a foreign land (Ex 2) is now ready to surrender his previous goals and ideals for the sake of the God who calls him. He allows himself to be changed and initially even to be cut down to size (3:3, 5f.). But then he accepts God's plan completely and thus becomes the man to whom Israel owes its rescue, its existence, and its law.

But Moses' exceptional closeness to God and all the honors he has already received here in the dialogue and will repeatedly receive later on have not gone to his head. Even when his people sin he places himself at their side, despite the fact that he himself has not shared in the sin. He rejects God's offer to make a great new people from him, and he begs for forgiveness for them, even offering to be destroyed with them if they are not forgiven (Ex 32:9–14, 32). As a result, the unique judgment passed on him in Numbers 12:3 does not surprise us: "Now the man Moses was very humble, more so than anyone else on the face of the earth." This is the paradoxical result of the fact that, graced as he was beyond any other in the Old Testament, he dealt face to face with God in speech and vision (Nm 12:8).

The possibilities for actualizing this call of Moses in terms of present-day situations are numerous and have already been expressed or suggested to some extent in the interpretation. The task is to try to apply the experience of Moses (e.g., his twofold education, his guilt, his unbridled striving for uprightness, the way God shows himself to him, and so on) to one's own situation and to see or to ask what impulses Moses' experience shows that can be translated into one's own personal experience.

QUESTIONS FOR REFLECTION

The plight of the poor and oppressed gives God and Moses a strong motive for intervening. Do we grasp the suffering of the marginalized, the misery of millions? Are we familiar with the perhaps hidden distress of human beings around us? Do we let ourselves be moved by it and perhaps even be transformed by it?

The five objections of Moses reveal his difficulties with the mission. Do I likewise manage to express my resistances, doubts, inhibitions to God? In doing so, or in spiritual conversation, do I find enlightenment?

In 4:1 Moses counts on the unbelief of his fellow Israelites. How do I view the people to whom I am sent?

God's answer to Moses in 4:11 hints at possible obstacles. Can we, even with our weaknesses and hindrances, accept our call?

In accepting his call, Moses is changed; he must give up his previous way of life. Am I ready to renounce my old ideals and plans? What changes have God and his mission produced in me?

2

"Where Are All the Wonderful Deeds of God?"
The Fear of a Warrior

Judges 6

*T*he Bible has a sense of humor. Gideon, a coward, is called "mighty warrior" (v. 12). Someone who, humanly speaking, seems weak and of lowly origin can become a mighty hero for God and rescue an entire people. The appointment of Gideon demands faith in God's power despite the limitations and inadequacies found in everyone who is called.

Situation

An Israel under pressure in the premonarchic period, probably in the twelfth and eleventh centuries B.C., is the subject of the book of Judges. The stories in this book show how God repeatedly sent Israel judges/rescuers. Most of the time, as in this particular instance, the nation's plight is the result of a break with God. But after a period of distress God takes pity on the Israelites when they call upon him for help (v. 6). In our passage God even answers twice, first by sending a prophet to admonish them and rebuke them for their ingratitude and disobedience (vv. 7–10), and then by appointing Gideon (vv. 11–24) to defend them against the Midianites.

Gideon had famous predecessors. Just before him Deborah, a judge, and Barak, her commander, had liberated Israel from the control of Jabin, king of Canaan, and his commander, Sisera (Jgs 4f.). This deliverance took place in almost the same part of the country (the tribes of Zebulun and Naphthali are mentioned in 4:6

and 6:35). The scene, then, is the fruitful Plain of Jezreel, a choice location for battles. There too is the locality named Ophrah (which today cannot be identified) where the messenger of Yahweh appears to Gideon (6:11).

Our text is part of the Deuteronomistic history, which includes the books of Joshua, Judges, Samuel, and Kings and which seems to have been written in about the sixth century B.C., about 500 years later than the events reported here. More important than the names of the foreign peoples (in addition to the Midianites, the Amalekites and "people of the East" are named in 5:3, 33) is their behavior and its consequences. They destroy Israel's harvests so that it is impoverished (vv. 4, 6). "Midianites" thus stands for those human beings/powers that undermine the toil and yield of a foreign people. (Other pictures of the Midianites are given in Ex 2:15ff.; Nm 25:6ff.; 31.) Gideon is to deliver Israel from this kind of exploitation.

Structure

The description of Gideon's appointment uses many of the elements known to us from Exodus 3. Among them is a short setting of the scene at the beginning, the change from messenger to Yahweh during the appearance, and above all, the call pattern:

Reference to a distress:	"Why then has all this happened to us?" (v. 13)
Commission:	"Go…I hereby commission you" (v. 14)
Objection:	"But how can I deliver Israel?" (v. 15)
Assurance:	"I will be with you" (v. 16)
Sign:	"Show me a sign" (v. 17)

This pattern is applied in a special way in Judges 6. The opening salutation in verse 12 already uses the formula of a promise of support. The distress is presented from the viewpoint of Gideon in his answer to the messenger (v. 13). The sign is connected with a meal that, like a sacrifice, is consumed by fire and ends with the building of an altar (v. 24).

As in Exodus 3, the name given to the one who appears to Gideon changes. As there (and in Gn 18), so here it is unnecessary to think because of this that there were originally two different stories. What we have, rather, is two aspects that belong together. When the focus is on the manner of the appearance, the text speaks of a messenger/angel (e.g., at the beginning of v. 11f. or toward the end of vv. 20, 22). When, however, the focus is on the content because there is question of something utterly essential and decisive, the subject is usually Yahweh (vv. 14, 16, and the comforting pledge in v. 23). The shift from messenger to God himself enables the narrator to give weight and structure to his story. In the process, Gideon stands out in the book of Judges as the only human being directly addressed by Yahweh.

Interpretation

Tall, majestic trees (Jgs 6:11) had an aura even in ancient Israel. In many places they were regarded as holy and were sites of religious gatherings, especially for the worshipers of Baal, as is indicated in the continuation of the present story (vv. 25ff.). God's messenger thus betakes himself to a place of an illegitimate, alien faith. Nearby, in the seclusion of a winepress, Gideon, whose name means "The one who cuts down" (see 6:25–27; and could also be freely translated as "Old Campaigner" or "Old Warhorse"), is threshing wheat on his father's plot of land.

This anxious caution of Gideon contrasts with the words of the messenger when he appears in verse 12. There the assurance of help, which can also be understood as a greeting, is followed by the description of Gideon as "mighty warrior," which was also used of the Israelites as they took possession of the land (Jos 8:3; 10:7) and will be used again later on of Jephthah (Jgs 11:1). Gideon is thereby placed in the number of those who establish a homeland for others or protect that homeland against threats. One task of those who are called is to ensure this security in the land given by God.

Surprisingly, Gideon's objection in v. 13 is directed not at this form of address but at the preceding assurance. By changing the angel's words to "if the Lord is with us," he makes the assurance to himself into an assurance to the entire community and then points out how it contradicts the present situation. Gideon's reproachful questions, "Why then…?" and "Where are all his wonderful [earlier] deeds?" and his concluding interpretation of the situation, "But now the Lord has cast us off" (in contrast to the popular view, "Yahweh will not reject us"; e.g., 1 Sm 23:22), show him to be a man of critical mind who will challenge others. There are, indeed, more comfortable partners in dialogue, but few are more honest. A call does not mean that one must give up one's own thoughts.

Yahweh addresses this skeptical Gideon (this phrase occurs only here in the Old Testament) and commissions him (v. 14). The reference of "in this might of yours" is unclear. It may refer to the bodily strength shown in the threshing of the wheat or to the independence and inner strength implied in the objection raised in verse 13, or to both. In Hebrew verse 14 takes the form of a rhetorical question, but in the context it is to be translated as a corroboration: "I have certainly sent you!"

As he has previously in response to the angel's greeting (v. 13), Gideon again voices his misgivings (v. 15). He immediately raises two objections: his clan is the weakest in the tribe, and he himself is the least in his family. Given these weaknesses, he does not see how he can carry out God's commission of rescuing Israel. A person's origins (family, place) and position (within the brothers and sisters or in other relationships) continue to set their mark on a vocation. Many modes of behavior still reflect those earlier relationships. Those called are guided, often unconsciously, by early impressions. This is also the cause of many conflicts.

God answers Gideon with the strengthening promise of his assistance (v. 16). The lack of means and any inadequacies are made up for by the fact that God is with him. As a result, the superiority of the enemy is reduced. The two are evenly matched; they are on the same level ("as if they [the Midianites] were but one man," NIV).

The end of the request for a sign that follows in verse 17 is usually translated inaccurately: "that it is you who speak with me." But Gideon does not know who this "you" is. The text reads literally: "then give me a sign, you, who are speaking with me." This formulation leaves open the identity of Gideon's addressee. In both translations Gideon's aim is to protect himself—an attitude that is evidently typical of him. The threshing of wheat in the winepress (v. 11) is understandable in view of the threat from the Philistines, but it also attests to Gideon's need for security. Moreover, ensuing events confirm this trait: even after Gideon's clan and four tribes have gathered (6:34f.), he asks God for two further signs as guarantees of victory (vv. 36–40). There is no denying that this man, who outwardly is an energetic hero, is also interiorly timorous. Gideon is an example of a person being called who, despite his insecurity, is sent by God and as a result makes others more secure.

God accepts Gideon's request (v. 18) and waits for the gift to be brought. This gift consists of an abundant meal (v. 19), the amount of which corresponds exactly to that in Genesis 18:6 (1 *ephah* = 3 *seahs,* about 40 liters!). The foods intended for eating are used in a strange way: the broth is thrown away, God's messenger touches the remainder that is set before him, but only with his staff, and then everything goes up in flames (perhaps a link with Elijah's sacrifice on Carmel in 1 Kgs 18:30ff.).

"Rocks," "fire," and the sudden disappearance of the angel cause Gideon to recognize the divine character of the appearance (v. 22; on "rock" = God, see Pss 18:3, 32; 28:1, etc.) and produce in him a sense of dread: "Alas, Lord God!" Like Jacob (Gn 32:30) and Moses (Ex 3:6), he knows the perils of seeing God; but unlike the former two, he attaches this danger even to the encounter with God's messenger. When God encounters human beings, the meeting frequently includes the two aspects described. Often it is only afterward that the light dawns. Often too the encounter gives rise not only to joy but to fright as well.

Yet God does not intend to frighten. "Shalom"—peace, well-being, happiness—he says to Gideon in verse 23. The goal of God's encounter with us is not dread and death, but true life. Gideon immediately expresses this truth by building an altar (v. 24; see Abraham, Gn 12:7f., and especially 13:18, the very place where the divine appearance occurs later on). To this altar Gideon gives the name "Yahweh is shalom" ("The Lord is peace"). The new life given by God in this encounter becomes visible in a new place of worship and is meant to radiate peace and well-being to all who venerate this God.

Perspectives

Gideon's call displays a twofold contrast: first, between the power promised him by God (vv. 12, 14, 16) and his sense of his own weakness, which causes him not to trust himself and to look repeatedly for assurance; and second, between his perception of the situation as hopeless and God's vision of the imminent rescue. A call involves not only looking at one's own apprehensions but also allowing God to invite us to see things as he does. It is thus that a change takes place which leads, as it does here, to peace and well-being. When we see the world from God's perspective, many things fit together harmoniously.

But until that state is reached, there are clashes. Gideon's first task, to pull down the altar of Baal and cut down the sacred pole, the *asherah,* leads to conflict with his own people (6:25–32). Only the forceful intervention of his father (v. 31) saves Gideon from being killed. In the process, Gideon, who obviously has pulled back out of fear (v. 27), acquires the name "Jerubbaal" ("Let Baal contend against him," v. 32). In the next conflict, with the Midianites, fear returns (7:10f.). Gideon, the great liberator and uninhibited, aggressive warrior (6:13, 27, and especially Jgs 8), is familiar with the dark side of frequent struggles: fear. On the other hand, Judges 6—8 shows how God repeatedly builds up Gideon's confidence. He keeps his promise to be with Gideon. Today too, those called have the experience of God taking away their fear, answering their wishes, and waiting for them.

There are a number of typical elements connecting Judges 6 with Genesis 18 and Exodus 3, as well as with Judges 13. But unlike the stories of Abraham and Moses, there are dark shadows over Gideon at the end. He does indeed, in exemplary fashion, refuse the Israelites' request in 8:22–23 that he rule over them, saying instead that God is to be their ruler. In this we see at work the community-centered outlook already noted in the "us" of 6:13. But immediately after this refusal Gideon accepts jewelry as payment, makes a cult object of it (an ephod, 8:27), and thereby leads the people into idolatry. What began so hopefully with the destruction of the sanctuary of Baal and the victory over the Midianites (6:25ff., and Jgs 7) ends in retaliatory killing and further apostasy (8:16f., 27). One false dependence is exchanged for another, as so often happens in the course of history. Gideon the liberator is unable to preserve and sustain an originally pure undertaking. His course becomes increasingly like the course and the people he originally did battle against. Thus a vocation can in time turn into its opposite. The turning point at which this change takes place is a great external victory.

QUESTIONS FOR REFLECTION

Gideon's answer to the messenger in 6:13 is not a courteous agreement, a polite yes. He does not play a part, does not hide his critical attitude. Do I express my opinion honestly? Do I dare to bring my ideas openly into a dialogue even when they differ from those of the majority?

Gideon several times shows a strong desire to protect himself. What are my "securities"? How greatly am I dependent on them?

God builds up the confidence of fearful Gideon. Have I experienced a growth of confidence? How did it come about?

Gideon's vocation turns into its opposite after a success. Have I lost an original ideal? At what points must I be on guard not to lose my call?

3

A Mother's Wisdom
The Wife of Manoah

Judges 13

*P*ersons who are called do not drop from heaven. They grow up in a human environment that bears the impress first and foremost of their parents. The attitudes of parents are often the soil from which distinguished personalities spring. In the appointment of the mother of Samson, the Bible underscores the decisive role of parents and, in addition, shows how they can fulfill their responsibilities despite their weakness and deficiencies.

Situation

The Philistines were a seafaring people who came from Crete and settled on the southwestern Mediterranean coast of Palestine around 1200 B.C. This flat belt of land, together with the adjacent low hill country, the Shephelah, was a fertile region, and a conflict soon arose over it with the ambitious Israelites.

This background is reflected in Judge 13—16. The events are to be dated probably in the second half of the twelfth century B.C. Judges 13:1 describes the recent apostasy that occurred after the death of Abdon the Judge (12:13–15). The ensuing passage follows the pattern that is described in detail in Judges 2:11–19. The superiority of the enemy and the threat from them loom over the people as consequences of their turning away from Yahweh. But once again God takes pity and sends Israel a rescuer/judge for the twelfth time in the person of Samson.

Structure

Manoah, whose name means "repose," and his wife, who is not named, belong to the tribe of Dan, which had settled on the frontier with the Philistines, half-way between Jerusalem and the Mediterranean. In the description of this couple, the barrenness of the wife is emphasized by the use of two expressions (13:2).

This humanly hopeless situation serves as the opportunity and prelude for the appearance of the messenger (angel) of Yahweh to the wife (vv. 3–5), during which he promises her a son and obliges her to a life resembling that of the Nazirites. She tells her husband of what has happened (v. 6).

Manoah thereupon asks Yahweh for a second coming of this "man," and this is granted to him and a second time to his wife (v. 8f.). Only because she notifies her husband (v. 10) does the meeting between him and the messenger of Yahweh take place. This meeting begins with a lengthy dialogue (vv. 11–18), which is followed by the remarkable departure of the messenger (vv. 19–21) and two different reactions from the couple (v. 22f.).

The birth, naming, and youth of Samson in verses 24–25 tell of the fulfillment of the promise and conclude our passage.

Interpretation

In the manner customary at that time, the narrator's statement in verse 2 makes the woman responsible for her childlessness. In his surprising appearance, God's messenger touches on this ticklish subject right at the beginning of his discourse (v. 3). All the more then does the subsequent promise of a son burst through all human expectations, just as earlier in the case of the ancestral mothers, Sarah and Rachel (Gn 18:10; 30:22).

The promise is tied to instructions that have their basis in the special destiny of this child (v. 4f.). He is to be a Nazirite from the beginning of his life. But the obligations of a Nazirite, as set down in Numbers 6 (in the form of a voluntary dedication for a limited time), are here divided in an odd way between mother and son: she is to abstain from alcohol and anything unclean; the hair of his head is not to be cut. While Numbers 6 speaks only of uncleanness from contact with a corpse, Samson's mother is not even to eat anything unclean (probably a link with the prescriptions regarding food in Lv 11 or Dt 14). Both prohibitions have as their purpose to keep the individuals observing them from losing their special closeness to God and, in consequence, their holiness. Vocations have a prehistory; they can be codetermined by the attitudes of parents and the youthful behavior of those called. A closeness to God that is felt in that period can serve as the foundation of an entire later life.

The instruction to the mother that she is to lead a sober and ritually clean life during her pregnancy betrays a knowledge that the behavior of the mother affects her growing child. When a mother thus pays heed to her child from its conception on, she provides it with ideal conditions for its development. In the case of Samson, this care, along with the sign that he himself is to maintain, namely, not cutting the hair of his head, leads to a hitherto unparalleled strength. A life thus directed to God from its very outset has the power to liberate from the strongest enemies. Samson's life work (end of v. 5) marks the beginning of a process in which Israel will be able to free itself from the overpowering domination of the Philistines. It is only under David (2 Sm 8:1f.; 23:8–17) or even later that this task will be to some extent completed.

The woman's report to her husband in verse 6 begins, typically, with a description of the appearance of the man who has presented himself to her. She calls him "man/messenger of God," but is unable to give any indication of his origin or name. Her verbatim repetition in verse 7 of what was said to her communicates everything essential in the message. The only thing new is the addition of "to the day of his death," which is perhaps evidence of a mother's premonition (see Jgs 16).

The reaction of Manoah in verse 8 is astonishing. As though a promise were not enough, he asks God for a new manifestation and connects this with the request for instruction on the rearing of the child. The reader must ask: Did he not have complete confidence in his wife? True enough, the testimony of women was at that time not valid. And yet his prayer does assume that a son will be given to them. Did Manoah perhaps feel passed over by the appearance to his wife, so that along with the appearance to "us" he asks for another that includes himself? Or is he a perfectionist who wants to know everything in detail and in advance, who wants to do everything correctly, and who is therefore not satisfied with the information God has thus far given?

In any case, God allows himself (the only time in such commissioning scenes in the Old Testament) to be persuaded to a second coming (v. 9 with vv. 22f.). He chooses the time and place so as to find the woman once again alone. She has to inform her husband. Her haste (two verbs to describe this in v. 10) contrasts with the obvious leisureliness with which Manoah follows her out to the messenger in verse 11. His first question, which is superfluous after what has happened, shows him to be a man who wants assurance.

His further question in verse 12 about the rearing of the son differs verbally from the question in verse 8, but its purpose is the same. The messenger's answer in verses 13–14 shows that this question is likewise superfluous. As far as the content of his answer goes, he repeats exactly (the addition "anything that comes from the vine" is a detail taken from Nm 6:4) what he had already said to the woman at his first appearance. He also stresses the role of the woman by making her the subject of all the sentences and by the fact that there is no repetition of the expressions "razor" and "Nazirite to God," which were used of Samson in the first communication and would have been a real answer to Manoah's question. Not by a single word does the messenger refer either to Manoah or to the boy.

Despite this snub, Manaoh does not let the messenger off. As a hospitable man, he wants to issue a generous invitation. But this suggestion is likewise rejected and turned aside into the suggestion that a sacrifice be offered to God instead (v. 15f.). The last sentence in verse 16, in which the narrator mentions Manoah's ignorance as an excuse for him, is at the same time the first sympathetic remark about this man who suffers one disappointment after another.

Even the added, well-intentioned ("honor," v. 17) question about the messenger's name meets only with a counterquestion and a remark that reminds Manaoh of his human limitations (v. 18). Undaunted, Manoah accepts the invitation to offer a sacrifice, and as he does so, he experiences, along with his wife, the miraculous departure of the man, whom they now recognize to be a messenger of God (vv. 19–21).

This belated realization triggers in Manoah a fear of death because he equates the messenger with God himself (v. 22). But his wife is able to calm him with the remark that the entire incident has shown God's good will toward them (v. 23).

The final two verses describe the fulfillment of what had been foretold. The newborn child is given the name Samson, usually interpreted as "sunny" or "(man of the) sun." God's blessing and spirit already leave their mark on his turbulent youth. His future will not be any different.

Perspectives

Is Judges 13 the story of a call? Anyone looking for the usual form of such accounts or for a commission that lays claim to an entire life runs into difficulties with this singular passage. It does not, in the usual way, say that God sends a human being. And yet it has so many elements in common with the call of Gideon in Judges 6 that we regard it likewise as a call, in this case the commissioning of the mother of Samson. It has become the model for the calling of Mary in Luke 1. The author has obviously taken from chapter 6 of this same book the motifs of the appearance of Yahweh's messenger, the liberation of Israel, the sacrifice of a goat, the recognition after the disappearance, and so on, in order to show that despite the changed circumstances there is here too a call. In doing so, he has combined these various elements with the promise of a son to a woman and a description of her husband, thereby making the role of the parents central. Let us look at the commission given to them.

As became clear in the Interpretation, the woman, even though unnamed, is in the foreground in many respects. God communicates primarily with her. Although according to the mind of that time the "guilt" for her childlessness weighs upon her, she is loyal to her husband (the report, vv. 6f.; fetching him, v. 10f.; calming him, v. 23), even though he is clearly a difficult man. Without objection she obediently accepts the conditions attached to the Nazirite vow, which elsewhere is always voluntarily chosen. She accepts, in addition, the obligation to follow the laws of purity in eating. She lives by the religious traditions of Israel and is prepared to renounce herself for the sake of God, her child, and the liberation of the people. Here, as with Deborah (Jgs 4), we are in the presence of a great woman. Whatever good a child does in its later life often has its roots in its mother.

If our observations in the Interpretation were correct, the narrator does not put the father in so complimentary a light. Manoah is fundamentally a "worthy" man, whose aim is to do nothing wrong and to be entirely correct. But precisely this kind of subtle exercise of power leads to some characteristics that are not so easy for others to put up with. Instead of being grateful to God for the promise of a son, Manoah gets him to send his messenger a second time. This and the leisurely reaction (matching his name "Repose") to his wife who comes in haste (v. 10f.) awakens at least an impression that he does not always take her seriously. His desire to control things leads subsequently to a series of wrong steps, and the final remark in verse 22 makes him seem somewhat naive in comparison with his wife.

Yet amid these dubious traits some light shines out. His request that God would instruct them, the parents, about the rearing of their child expresses a never-ending longing of humanity:

mothers and fathers in every age learn from experience that the rearing of their children is fundamentally a task that is beyond them. Manoah's prayer is the perpetual cry of parents who really love their children. At the same time, Manoah's constant friendly comfortableness is not a bad setting for the growth of a young man in whom the spirit "stirs" (v. 25). Even after three millennia, patience seems to be as necessary now as it was then.

The very next chapter, Judges 14, shows the choice of a bride as a classical family conflict. What human being will know his or her way around amid the confusing play of clashing forces, amid pressures and betrayals, arrogance and naiveté, loss and gain? For Samson's parents the situation is as impenetrable as it would be later on for the prophet Hosea, who at God's bidding marries a prostitute (Hos 1:2f.). Yet just as his barren mother, of all people, bore him, the strong liberator, so Samson too lives until his death (Jgs 16) amid great tension, torn as he is between his attraction to Philistine women and his unbridled urge to rescue his people from this enemy. Even in the baffling mysteries of our world God's plan is brought to fulfillment.

The institution of Naziritism is both supported and adapted in Judges 13. On the one hand, the divine commission legitimatizes this way of life in a manner that goes beyond Numbers 6 and ascribes an immense liberating power to it. On the other hand, it is applied to the time of pregnancy as being a desirable form of precaution. The sobriety and purity of his mother (to the extent that the observance of the prescriptions for eating are linked to an inner attitude) leave Samson to grow up unencumbered and undamaged. Today these interior attitudes and a corresponding outward life are still great gifts that a mother can make to her children even before their birth.

QUESTIONS FOR REFLECTION

How did my mother mold me? How did my father?

How do we regard our task as parents?

A vocation very often means burdens for our parents and our brothers and sisters; often too, it leads to alienation and remoteness. Do we understand what they endure for us?

God's conduct urges us to the equal and just treatment of women. What role(s) do I play in the relationship between the sexes?

In what ways do I experience sober alertness and resolute purity as sources of strength? What does "pure" mean to me?

4

The Voice in the Night
Young Samuel

1 Samuel 3

*T*his can't turn out well, one might think. Here is a child at a
very tender age being thrust by his mother into a career as a priest.
Moreover, conditions in the temple in which he is to serve are
repellent, in fact, a perversion of faith. Samuel's vocation shows
how even in such adverse circumstances God achieves his purpose. This is reason for hope, especially in what many see as a
muddled situation in the church.

Situation

Around the middle of the eleventh century B.C., the Israelite
tribes were faced with a dilemma. They had previously maintained
their independence as small scattered groups and had led lives that
although very simple were nevertheless independent. The growing
pressure from the Philistines and other neighboring national states
(Ammon, Moab) has forced them to unite. Now by their combined
forces they are able to defend themselves against hostile attacks.
The first but still unsuccessful attempt at union was the monarchy
of Saul, but after him Israel under David managed to develop a
state that was to last for a good four hundred years.

Samuel lived through this historical change and influenced
it at key points. He was the last of the judges (1 Sm 7:15), serving
as the "midwife" at this transition from the tribal Israel of the
prenational period to a monarchically constituted state. Even
though the establishment of kingship came about against his will

(8:6ff.), Israel nonetheless owed to Samuel its continued existence as a nation.

Even Samuel's prehistory was a turbulent one. In 1 Samuel 1 we learn of the feud between Peninnah and Hannah, the two wives of his father, Elkanah. Hannah was more loved by her husband, but she had thus far remained childless and was for this reason exposed to Peninnah's snide remarks. In her distress she prayed and vowed that if she should have a son she would give him to Yahweh for his entire life (1 Sm 1:11). Thus Samuel's destiny was decided even before he had been conceived. Because Hannah prayed silently, perhaps because she felt neglected and bitter, Eli the priest thought she was drunk (vv. 12–15).

When Hannah gives birth, she gives the child the name Samuel, the meaning of which in Hebrew can no longer be explained with certainty (1:20; the meaning "I have asked for him" fits Saul rather than Samuel). She keeps him for a good three years until he is weaned. Then, faithful to her promise, this woman filled with praise of God, brings little Samuel to Eli in Shiloh, thirty kilometers north of Jerusalem, the national religious sanctuary where the ark of the covenant is kept, and leaves him there (1:20—2:11).

Contrary to all fearful expectations, this young child, who has been taken much too soon from his family, flourishes splendidly, thanks in part to further maternal care (2:18f., 26). Thus Samuel distinguishes himself in a very positive way from the sons of Eli, who, despite being priests and despite Eli's fatherly exhortations, do not refrain from unbridled gluttony, corrupt use of their office, and sexual misconduct (2:12–17, 22, 25). Their lack of understanding moves God to take back his promise to the priestly house of Aaron (2:30; see Ex 29:9). The obstinacy of Eli's sons in their evil ways has brought him and his house to a dead end. How will God act from now on?

Structure

1 Samuel 3 answers this question with the call of Samuel. The verb *call* plays a more dominant role here than in any other Old Testament call story. Correspondingly, Samuel shows himself as a youngster who is an eager listener. He becomes God's confidant and the new recipient of God's word.

1 Samuel 3:1–3 sets the scene. This is followed in verses 4–9 by something unique in the Bible: a prelude that might also be called a "calling game" and that serves to delineate further the persons involved. Verse 10 forms the conclusion of this game and leads to verses 11–14, the divine message given to Samuel and intended for Eli. In verses 15–18, after a short dialogue between Eli and Samuel, the message is passed on. The final three verses (19–21) tell how Samuel grows increasingly into his role as hearer of the divine word and as prophet. In verse 19 we find the assurance familiar to us from the call pattern: "The Lord was with him."

Interpretation

Samuel is still young. He is God's servant, but under the supervision of Eli (3:1; compare 2:11). Despite human inadequacies and dependencies his dedication is to God himself, even though he has not yet come to know the Lord personally (v. 7). This lack of knowledge is not surprising in a setting in which the word of God or the vision of God has become rare (v. 1)—perhaps even precisely because children (Eli's sons) no longer listen to their parents (2:25).

Eli, the priest of Shiloh, is old and has also become almost blind. He is asleep in his place outside the temple (v. 2), while inside Samuel, near the ever-burning lamp, is carrying out his duty by sleeping near the ark of God (v. 3). Despite his youth, Samuel has in fact already taken over Eli's duty. His is the role of keeping watch and protecting the temple. Just so, small, simple tasks in the church or community (e.g., servers, youth leaders) are often a preparation for and an introduction to a later life of selfless dedication. By way of such services young people grow into their own responsible positions. It is in this way that they also acquire confidence and courage for generous decisions.

Verses 4–10 play on the fact that the reader already knows that God is the one calling, whereas Eli and Samuel only slowly come to realize this. In this perspective, Samuel's first answer, "Here I am!" in verse 4 sounds like that of a person who awakes from sleep and does not yet grasp what is happening. He nevertheless runs to Eli, who sends him back to his sleep (v. 5). The second occurrence shows slight changes (v. 6): Samuel goes to Eli immediately without responding to God's call and reports to him as before. Eli obviously recognizes the boy's disquiet and confusion. With the address "my son," which is an addition as compared with verse 5—Samuel is his son not by blood but by his attitude and position—Eli comforts and calms him before sending him back to sleep again.

In order to keep the listener/reader from false conclusions, the narrator introduces Samuel's inexperience as an explanation (v. 7). The boy could not know who was calling him. It is all the more surprising, then, that even after the two "failures," after twice rising vainly in the night, at the third call an unflustered Samuel again reports to Eli, who this time understands (v. 8). This time, before the boy returns to sleep, the old priest gives him a suitable answer should he hear the call again: "Speak, Lord, for your servant is listening" (v. 9).

Because God comes and stands there, and because the call is repeated: "Samuel, Samuel!" (compare Ex 3:4), the beginning of verse 10 has a much more solemn character than the previous calls. From this moment, in which the young Samuel is capable of answering him in an appropriate way, God speaks to him personally. As in other such calls, this leads to a turning point in his life. In response to God's urgent summons, Samuel repeats the answer given him by Eli, but probably out of timidity, he omits the divine name, Yahweh (Lord).

In the next four verses (11–14) God makes Samuel the confidant of his intention. He tells him of the end of Eli's priestly family. In verse 11 the phrase "ears tingle" heralds the incredible and dreadful nature of the coming events (described in 1 Sam 4f.). Verse 12 alludes to the fact that Eli has already been warned (in 2:30ff.). The crux of the reproach brought against him is that he knew of the actions of his sons and did not effectively put a stop to them (v. 13; see also 2:23–25). As is so often the case, a lenient parental "love" that tolerates the faults of growing children leads inevitably to ruin (v. 14).

God's message puts Samuel in a bind. Can he convey this fearful news to Eli, when the latter has been his fatherly protector and great religious teacher? After such a night Samuel's fear as he opens the doors in the morning is understandable (v. 15). Eli himself eases the tension of this uncomfortable situation by his benevolent familiarity ("Samuel, my son," v. 16) and by his demand for radical honesty ("hide nothing," twice in v. 17). Samuel obeys and thus at the same time carries out God's intention (v. 18; in v. 13, "I have told him"). Eli's reaction is remarkably composed. It attests to a profound trust in God.

The final three verses describe Samuel's further career. The Lord stands by him and faithfully carries out everything he says (none of his words "fall to the ground," v. 19; see also 2 Kgs 10:10), so that all, from the farthest north to the deepest south ("from Dan to Beersheba," v. 20), acknowledge Samuel to be a trustworthy spokesman for Yahweh. God himself maintains his familiar closeness to Samuel at Shiloh through appearances and messages (v. 21). It has been a long journey from God's first call at the beginning to a continuous activity as a "prophet" who is acknowledged by the people. God unceasingly accompanies this development and keeps trust with those who represent him.

Perspectives

The "calling game" (vv. 4–9) is a literary jewel. It shows Samuel as a zealous servant who rises up straightaway in the night in response to every call, even after mistakes or deceptions. God chooses this individual despite his youth and lack of experience. The important thing is not so much intelligence or a great name as a ready, serving, listening heart.

God does not force himself on Samuel but allows him to make the discovery himself, like a wise teacher who knows that discoveries made by students take them further than the brilliant performances of their elders. God does not trample on Samuel. With great patience and with understanding of the boy's ignorance, God allows him time and accepts the risk that the call may be misunderstood. In fact, Samuel thrice mistakes God's call for the call of his human teacher, Eli. Still today, a divine call is often mistakenly identified with the claims of secular or ecclesiastical authority. But as is made clear here, God's authority can wait and take human freedom seriously.

The "calling game" is a wonderful example of the relationship of young and old. In his lack of experience, Samuel is dependent on Eli, whose insight and knowledge of God have matured over long years. The old and the traditional, even when perhaps outdated, retain a role, that of leading to God young people who are ready to listen and of opening them to experience of him. In this passage Eli and Samuel play their parts in the education of faith in an exemplary way. Eli is even able to accept criticism of himself (v. 18). The classical generational conflict is thus seen in a different light: real problems arise when people do not listen (2:25). On the other hand, readiness to learn from one another and mutual respect create a climate of trust in which even the traditional priestly nobility and young people pointing out its mistakes can come together with good will.

This is not easy for young Samuel. Such a situation brings him into conflict with his commitments and his feelings. It is from Eli that he has learned what faith is. From his earliest youth this priest has been father and friend to him. Yet now the boy is to advance beyond him. On God's behalf he must tell him of his downfall. Eli's greatness shows itself here in the way in which he guesses the young man's difficult situation and helps him: honesty alone saves (v. 17). Love tells the truth, even when it hurts. Samuel, for his part, opens himself to a man whose mistaken leniency has promoted corruption and thus brought on his fall. This kind of openness is utterly essential for those who are called. If a person cannot or will not make his inner self known, his witness to God will likewise remain incomplete.

1 Samuel 3 portrays a person growing into his mission as few other call stories do. Samuel, who has been destined for God by his mother, grows increasingly into a personal, authentic dedication of his life to God. After he has carried out external tasks in the temple and while he still lacks a personal knowledge of God, his first encounter with Yahweh becomes the decisive, crucial experience. But this alone is not enough; also needed is its continuation in subsequent daily life. Honest, courageous proclamation, intimacy with God, and acceptance by the people turn Samuel into the great personality who for a long time to come leaves God's impress on Israel. The initial determination by another that he is to serve God has changed to an abiding personal commitment of his own. It is similarly important for those called today that the part played by outsiders be clarified and, if it is unauthentic, that it be renounced in favor of new, authentic motivations for a personal acceptance of a mission. Spiritual exercises, spiritual companionship, novitiates, and seminaries serve in this process; but the process lasts a lifetime.

The time of radical change within which Samuel and the entire people are living does not spare even him from painful experiences. The defeat by the Philistines leads to the loss of the ark of the covenant and to the death of his teacher, Eli (1 Sm 4).

Samuel himself has to endure the same experience with his sons that Eli did before him (1 Sm 8:2f.). It is the corruption of these sons that gives rise among the Israelites to the demand for a king. Saul, the first king whom he anoints, turns out increasingly to be unfit (beginning in 1 Sm 13); and Samuel fearfully anoints Saul's successor, David (1 Sm 16:2, 13). The thing that keeps Samuel going through all these difficult times is his openness to God, who at critical moments points him toward God's different paths (1 Sm 8:6f.; 9:15–17; 16:6f.). In listening to God, Samuel receives the keys to the future.

QUESTIONS FOR REFLECTION

Hannah arranges things for Samuel. Are there, in my case as well, "foreign," unclarified influences in my vocation? Am I nonetheless able, like Samuel, to turn a life in the service of God into my own personal commitment?

Hannah gives her son as a very young child to the service of God. She must forego having him near her and, later on, having his help. Are we aware of what renunciations and sacrifices our vocation entails for our closest relatives and friends? In what ways do we ease this loss and pain for them?

Samuel serves the Lord in the temple without knowing him. How much interior intimacy do I have with God?

Samuel is a model by reason of his readiness to serve, even in the night and after failures. Can our dedication, our commitment, stand comparison with his? Am I able to make myself free for the call of God?

Samuel needs Eli's help in his vocation. Have others helped us by means of their experience? Are we open to letting ourselves be led, in faith, by older people?

Samuel's first task demands that he be radically honest with Eli. Am I likewise driven by a sense of responsibility toward God's word and the truth? Can I open myself to this?

5

A Stranger's Mantle
Elisha, Successor of Elijah

1 Kings 19

A well-to-do farmer who gives up everything, and this at the call of a human being—this is what Elisha's call shows us. Hitherto, the call always came directly from God; here for the first time, the call to Elisha is mediated by a human being who makes an unconditional claim. In issuing this call, Elijah combines in a strange way harsh, barely understandable traits with a profound grasp of the heavy consequences that his call to follow has for Elisha. The calls of the disciples in the New Testament are entirely in this tradition.

Translation of 1 Kings 19:19–21

[19] And he went away from there, and he found Elisha, the son of Shaphat, and the latter was plowing at the time. Twelve yoke of oxen were in front of him, and he was with the twelfth. And Elijah passed by him and threw his mantle over him.
[20] Then he left the oxen and ran after Elijah and said: "I want to kiss my father and my mother, then I will go after you." And he said: "Go! Turn back, for what have I done to you?"
[21] Then he turned back from behind him and took the yoke of oxen, slaughtered it, and using the vessels of the oxen, he cooked the flesh, and he gave to the people, and they ate. Then he rose up, went after Elijah, and served him.

Situation

In the middle of the ninth century B.C., under King Ahab, the northern kingdom was restless, both politically and religiously. The country had to endure the tensions between the Canaanite and the Israelite populations with their different conceptions of justice (e.g., Naboth's vineyard in 1 Kgs 21) and their clashes over beliefs (see 1 Kgs 18, the divine judgment on Carmel). In addition, there were—probably to an even greater degree at a later period—disagreements with Aram, a neighboring state (e.g., 1 Kgs 20; 2 Kgs 5ff.), about claims to possession of the land of Gilead, east of the Jordan.

On the border with Gilead, but on the western bank of the Jordan in the tribal territory of Issachar, lay Abel-meholah, where Elisha lived. Another opinion places this locality in Gilead itself. Previous conflicts have led to threats on Elijah's life by Queen Jezebel (1 Kgs 19:2). Only by fleeing to Mount Horeb has Elijah escaped her vengeance. There, after a divine manifestation that questions his zeal, he receives his commission to anoint three different individuals (v. 15f.).

The anointing of Elisha as Elijah's successor is God's answer to the danger threatening Elijah and to the attempt to silence his powerful divine word. No matter what may happen to Elijah, in the future Elisha will carry on his mission and the divine message.

Structure

1 Kings 19:19–21 is unique in the Old Testament, inasmuch as in it one human being calls another. The only parallels are in the calls of the disciples in the New Testament. In particular, there is such a striking resemblance between this passage and the calls of the disciples in Mark 1 and 2 that the latter may be regarded as dependent, from a literary point of view, on 1 Kings 19 (see below, Chapter 11). What these texts have in common can be represented by a pattern containing eight elements:

	1 Kings 19	**Mark 1:16–20**	**Mark 2:13–16**
1. Verbs of motion	went	passed by	passed by
2. Meeting	found	saw	saw
3. Work	plowing	fishing	fishing
4. Call	throwing mantle over him	"Follow me!"	"Follow me!"
5. Surrender of work	left	left	getting up
6. Following	ran	immediately followed	followed
7. Parting from parents	father, mother	left father	
8. Eating	meal for the people		eating with sinners

The first element shows the callers (Elijah, Jesus) on their way. Next (2), there is a meeting ("find" is also used at the call of Philip in Jn 1:43). This meeting shows those called at their usual work (3). They are called away from this (4) by the gesture of Elijah or the command of Jesus. Those called respond immediately, break off their activity (5), and follow the one who makes such a powerful claim on them (6); the Greek verb, even in the Septuagint, is always *akoloutheô,* "follow." The new way of life demands the surrender of existing ties, which takes place in the parting from parents (7) and present friends, and with a meal (8).

In view of the extensive agreement among the three texts in their sequences and choice of words, we can speak of a pattern and, on the basis of the key word found in the sixth element, describe it as a "call to following." The call demands a radical change of life as made visible in the unheard of giving up of one's daily work, in the call itself, and in the parting from one's closest intimates. At the same time, the call is a very human event from meeting to parting. It leaves room for emotions and brings the one parting into a new closeness and sense of community with the caller. The surprising thing in all this is the absolute, unchallenged authority of those who so bluntly call others to a following that has such serious consequences.

Interpretation

Obeying the instructions of Yahweh (v. 15f.), Elijah leaves Horeb and meets Elisha. Like Moses and Gideon before him, Elisha is engaged in a rural activity that symbolically anticipates his later work. As he plows the soil in order to make it fruitful once again, so as follower of Elijah he will cultivate the people and the king in order that they may bear fruit through orthodox faith. The twelve yoke signify not only a prosperous family but also all of Israel with its twelve tribes. Despite all the differences, there is also a continuity between earlier activity and mission. As with Elisha, so with many who are called, the past and the work done in it leave a positive mark on later activity.

Unexpectedly, and to his complete surprise, Elisha suddenly finds himself in the dark. The stranger's mantle deprives him of vision and lays a tremendous claim on him: Elijah demands that he follow him. Elijah's mantle had served him in an important way at his encounter with God (v. 13), and again at his definitive departure (2 Kgs 2) it will symbolize his spirit and power. The completely new idea of entering the service of God and, in addition, the beginning of a relationship of dependency on another human being (in Elisha's case, until Elijah is taken away) can obscure one's outlook and be felt as a burden. In the beginning, a call is not "pure bliss." It often takes a long time before the gaze is really free and the mantle of responsibility and discipleship no longer weighs heavily.

The gesture of throwing one's mantle, which is attested only here, is understood by Elisha, and the claim it makes is immediately accepted. Elisha even runs after Elijah, who has evidently kept going and not waited. Elisha asks permission to take leave of his people at home. The verb *kiss* emphasizes, in addition, the emotions Elisha is feeling (see also the reaction of Laban when Jacob departs from him, Gn 31:28; 32:1). Elijah grants this in a kind of admission: "For what have I done to you?" In the Bible, such formulas are always connected with guilt or burdensome relations (e.g., Gn 20:9; 31:26); the closest formulation is in Numbers 22:28, in the innocent donkey's words to Balaam, who has struck it. A delicate element in vocations is addressed with matchless brevity: on the one hand, there is the necessary detachment from family and earlier ties, and on the other, this process requires a great deal of tact, especially on the part of superiors, and open space for emotions. If this development is suppressed, the mission can be burdened or hindered.

The departure from his family takes place in a different and fuller way than Elisha had requested. There is a real feast to which not only his parents but many others ("the people") come for a good meal. The slaughtering and burning of work animals and tools shows Elisha's firm determination to give up his former career. The well-to-do farmer, who has twelve yoke of oxen "in front of him" (v. 19: signifying control?), turns into a servant, who goes *after* Elijah (*after* occurs 4 times in vv. 20f.). This reflects the experience of so many who give up a profession to follow a call. Whatever they were previously undergoes a period of transformation that is accompanied by feelings of powerlessness, failure, and insignificance.

Perpectives

This account of Elisha's call is gripping in its brevity. In fact, Elisha's immediate readiness and his zeal (he not only "goes" but "runs") in response to a gesture is astonishing. Without any prior testing or lengthy reflection being mentioned, he lets himself in on the spot for a radical break in his life, and this solely on Elijah's authority, claimed over him by a prophetic gesture. The question remains whether and to what extent Elisha was previously acquainted with this Elijah whom he now follows. The text is not calling a man to rash decisions but is emphasizing Elijah's authority and Elisha's exemplary freedom in surrendering himself. Down to our own day, the prompt and eager responses of those called are often a cause of astonishment. With generosity and courage they let themselves in for a radical break in their lives. This bears witness not only to the power of the call but also to the magnanimity of those who follow and their great trust in the caller.

God's commission was to "anoint" Elisha. We do not learn whether this anointing took place. In any case, the way in which Elijah here calls upon Elisha to follow him marks only the beginning of a lengthy shared journey on which Elisha truly becomes a follower. We know only the beginning and the end (2 Kgs 2) of the journey. In the course of it, the decisive role, over and above the physical community, is played by Elisha's sharing in the "spirit" of Elijah, that is, in his closeness to God, with all the concrete effects of this. Elisha receives the spirit of his teacher by accompanying him, loyally and unwaveringly, to the last moment of his life.

The long, hidden years that Elisha spent in the service of Elijah have their counterpart today in a formation that usually lasts for several years. It is not easy for many who are called to endure these dragging years without any personal responsibility for others. Yet in the endurance of seeming meaninglessness and uselessness, a loving commitment can become strong, provided the fire of desire to serve burns within.

In the New Testament, Jesus will call human beings to follow him with comparable authority but in an even more radical way (see Lk 9:59–62). Like Elisha, those called will continue his work. In this way God sees to it that his message does not disappear and that his saving action continues to reach humanity. Over and over, God has sent new followers to those he has called. Even if individual orders or forms of religious life die out, his call is nonetheless heard even at the present time by persons who gladly follow and thereby take their place in the immense line of his messengers that runs through the entire history of the world.

QUESTIONS FOR REFLECTION

What role can other persons play in vocations?

To whom do we owe our present way of life?

What replaces the throwing of the mantle in our day?

Consider Elisha's immediate decision to make a radical break: How great is our readiness to change?

Why is there an anxiety and reluctance to speak to others about a life of discipleship?

6

"Whom Can I Send?"
Unclean in the Presence of the Divine

Isaiah 6

Who wants to accept a commission that is condemned in advance to failure or even produces the opposite of what is desired? Isaiah's call, which brings us into the realm of the great writing prophets, faces him with such a "meaningless" mission. His call springs from an encounter with the sublimely holy God, who transcends all human representations, who cleanses human beings from guilt and thereby liberates them for eager generosity. The radiant power of this call text reaches even into the eucharistic celebration in the "Holy, holy, holy" of the seraphim and the greeting of the "Lord of hosts." The confession of guilt and cleansing from it are also found in Isaiah 6.

Situation

Isaiah 6:1 locates the entire chapter in the year of Uzziah's death (ca. 736 B.C.); 7:1 provides the next date, the reign of Uzziah's grandson Ahaz. Uzziah, also known as Azariah, was assigned an exceptionally long reign of fifty-two years. But he fell ill with leprosy, and probably for this reason, his son Jotham took over the business of governing. (For the entire story, see 2 Kgs 15:1–17.)

When Isaiah 6:5 gives God the title of "king," the passage is mindful of what is going on behind the scenes: the death of the elderly, sick king of Judah, whose sickness has isolated him and made him no longer capable of reigning. In contrast to the tensions and unrest often connected with the deaths of earthly rulers (2 Kgs 11 provides an example), God's reign remains inviolable and unshakable.

This superiority of God shines out in Isaiah 6. Many details in the opening verses of our passage reflect God's sovereignty. In his vision Isaiah sees the temple, but God's manifestation surpasses the building's dimensions. By the way in which they act, the seraphim confirm God's superiority to them. Yahweh not only transcends everything human; but even in the heavenly, divine sphere he alone is sovereign. The temple of Jerusalem, the place to which Isaiah's vision is tied and the center of religion in Judah, is only a weak reflection of this God whose glory fills the entire world.

Structure

Isaiah 6 can be divided into three parts:

vv. 1–4   the vision of the Holy One
vv. 5–7   the purifying fire
vv. 8–11 the sending of Isaiah

The final two verses (12f.) lead the gaze further into the dark future, but they speak of Yahweh in the third person and, in the final sentence, allow a suggestion of hope and confidence. Many interpreters regard these two verses as an addition made in the exilic period. As verse 11 effects a transition to verses 12–13, which belong with it in theme, so the vision of Yahweh in verse 5 is connected by the key word *see* with what follows.

A careful reading of the text allows us to see elements of the call pattern although there are transpositions:

v. 5   "I am a man of unclean lips"   —objection
vv. 6f.   Touching of lips with a live coal   —sign
vv. 8f.   "Whom shall I send?…Go and say!"   —commission

The missing elements—"reference to distress" and "assurance"—can be seen in the context: the approach of the Assyrians (5:26–30) and the overwhelming vision of Yahweh in 6:1–4. Anyone who has had such a profound experience of God needs no external corroboration.

The transposition of the elements that we see here is unique and significant. Only here does God's commission come in last place, only here is it formulated as a question (but see 1 Kgs 22:20), and only here does it meet with a voluntary, unconditional declaration of readiness from the one being sent. This shift is made possible by the objection being put first (v. 5). The admission of guilt and the cleansing from it prepare the way for the unlimited acceptance of the divine commission. Isaiah is the only one who puts himself forward and declares his readiness for a mission from God.

Both aspects are important today. Those being called must not be blind to their guilt. It is precisely the admission of their own sinfulness that intensifies their solidarity with the sinful people, allows God to respond in a healing way by purifying them, and creates the presuppositions required for the mission. The experience of God's liberating from sin supports many a vocation. As it does here with Isaiah, it makes possible a voluntary tender of oneself. The person who thus encounters God's unmerited forgiveness is able in turn to give himself totally and freely to God. God's mercy lights the fire of readiness in his messengers.

Interpretation

Isaiah 6:1 provides the first dating of a text in the book. This is another reason why, even though five chapters precede, the incident described here is to be understood as the call of Isaiah at the beginning of his public activity. The undated texts that precede it display, on the one hand, God's very great generosity and care (Is 1:18; 2:1–5; 4:2–6; 5:1f.), but, on the other hand, show any corresponding human response to be lacking (1:21ff.; 2:6ff.; 5:4ff.). The first five chapters thus make vivid the hardening of the people despite the divine offer of favor and thereby make intelligible the strange commission given to Isaiah (see below on vv. 9f.).

The "Lord" seen here on a throne is the God who is in repose and who exercises dominion from a sedentary position. God's exalted (two adjectives) place is further emphasized by the statement that the train or even just the hem of the royal robes fills the temple, which was almost fifteen meters high. This God transcends human measures and images.

The six-winged seraphim (v. 2; the Hebrew word originally describes serpents) who surround and serve God are a familiar element taken over from the surrounding ancient oriental world. In Egypt the cobra, as a protective power, was on the front of the pharaoh's crown, and was represented on seals that show winged serpents, though with only two or four wings.

In Egypt the seraphim/serpents took their place as a protective power over the king, who was venerated as a god. But they appear in Isaiah 6 in a considerably reinterpreted role: they are beings that belong to the divine world but are themselves in need of protection. With the extra pairs of wings (above and beyond the pair needed for flying) they hide their faces and their private parts ("feet"): the former in order not to be endangered by the sight of God (see Jgs 13:22), the latter as sign of their nakedness and vulnerability. Both gestures emphasize the majesty of God in whose service they are.

Their calls (v. 3) heighten this majesty even further. They confess aloud and bear witness, each to the others, to God's supreme holiness and glory that fills the world. In Hebrew the threefold repetition, "Holy, holy, holy," expresses the highest degree of intensification. It signifies that in abiding purity and perfection God is far removed from the sinfulness of humanity and the world and their subjection to sin. Such holiness belongs in an unsurpassable degree to "Yahweh Sabaoth." The epithet *Sabaoth,* "of armies," refers to the heavenly army, probably the stars, which at an earlier time were also venerated as gods. Even among them the role of leader belongs to Yahweh. But God's power is not limited to heaven; in the form of a radiant force ("glory"), it fills the entire earth. This power shows itself immediately in verses 4–5. The cries of the seraphim alone are enough to shake the great temple to its foundations and fill it with smoke (a sign of the divine presence; e.g., Ex 19:18).

If even the seraphim hide their faces from God, how much more must Isaiah do so, being a sinful human being! As a result, he thinks that he is lost (v. 5). He twice speaks of "unclean lips," a phrase met only here in the Old Testament. The lips are the instruments of speech. Elsewhere in Isaiah they also have an important function (11:4; 37:29), or serve to deceive (29:13; 59:3). The closest passages in other books are the "uncircumcised lips" of Exodus 6:30, and the "perverse lips" of Proverbs 4:24. With their lips human beings form a connection between thought and action when they speak. But if these lips are unclean or lying, how can there be any good in a person? Much less can such a condition exist in the presence of Yahweh, "the king."

The lives of God's messengers experience such overwhelming moments from time to time. God reveals himself to them in the otherness of his incomprehensible goodness and all-embracing immensity. This experience is often combined with a sense of the individual's complete unworthiness. To those who are called, the gift is given of seeing God in his infinite distance from human transiency and lowliness and yet at the same time of surrendering themselves to him.

But this God wants not to destroy but to cleanse (v. 6ff.). With a live coal taken from the altar (of incense?), a seraph touches the lips of Isaiah and explains the gesture as signifying the distancing or, as the case may be, the covering over of guilt and sin. "Covering over" is not to be understood as a hiding that glosses over, a hushing up, but as a compensatory repayment or admission of guilt, so that it no longer exists and is no longer counted against the person. At an earlier time, people cauterized wounds and thus made possible the subsequent growth of healthy tissue. In like manner, the purification from guilt can be connected with fiery pain, for example in the realization of how much others have suffered from one's sin.

In verse 8 the Lord begins to speak, not demanding but questioning, not highhandedly but referring to a community ("us," the beings, named several times in this passage, who belong to God's sphere). Since Isaiah has already been purified, he is able to declare himself ready, without reservations, without objections based on his unworthiness or inability, and to beg God: "Here I am! Send me!" When God's inquiry encounters such a generous human yes (Lk 1:38 is a fine example), God is able to make full use of the addressee for the salvation of humanity.

That is what happens here in a surprising, even shocking way. The prophet is entrusted with the commission of telling the people to listen but at the same time not to understand (vv. 9f., cited in Mt 13:14f. with reference to the inability of Jesus' hearers to understand his parables). In a provocative way, God foretells a failure to understand. Even the intense effort of the people to understand (the absolute infinitive is used twice in the Hebrew text) is bound to fail. In addition, Isaiah has the task of impairing the people's ability to listen (v. 10: "make the heart obese, make the ears heavy, paint the eyes closed"), so that they may not be converted and saved.

What is God's purpose? The "failure" of Isaiah's mission is, as it were, programmed in advance. Just as in the passages that have preceded (Is 1—5) the people have already often rejected God's concern for them, so they will also react with stubbornness later on (7:11ff.; 8:5ff.; 9:12ff.; in addition, compare 28:7ff. and 29:9ff.). Isaiah's commission is executed in spite of its failure. Resistance and "obese hearts" among the people (what a splendid image for the consequences of prosperity and self-satisfied affluence!) not only spring from human selfishness but are also a part, at least provisionally, of God's plan.

Persons in many countries of the world who are called have comparable experiences. Even today admonishing voices are not popular. Anyone standing up for God's purposes, ethical values, obedience to law, justice for the poor, the preservation of creation, and so on attacks the interests of certain influential groups that react with rejection and resistance, often mercilessly.

In response to Isaiah's question about the duration of his mission (v. 11), God reveals his further purpose. The obduracy is limited in time and will end when the land is laid waste and empty of people. Verses 12–13 explain that this condition is due to everyone's "being sent away" (the reference is probably to the Exile) and to the renewed wasting or burning of the remaining tenth. But our passage ends with an image that is full of trust. The remnant that is left by this purification is not a dead stump (see also 11:1), but a "holy seed" and therefore like him, the holy God. This conciliatory conclusion is not a happy ending, but it does give confidence. However bad social situations may be, God's ways make it possible for human beings to be increasingly like him.

Perspectives

First of all, Isaiah's instructions, which are unintelligible to many and announce a failure to understand, need further explanation. Isaiah 6 is part of a redaction that, in a first-person form, looks back from a later time to the public appearance of this prophet and to the failure to accept his message and in this way integrates his call into the context of the book as a whole and of the following chapters in particular. It thus makes clear that this human rejection was foreseen by God and even—the word must be used cautiously—willed by him, because in this way, by means of a purifying judgment, a new people can arise that is united to him. God thus retains a concern for his people, and Isaiah's mission is a visible expression of the fact that the human beings he has made matter to him, even though the opposition between himself, the utterly Holy One, and humanity with its "unclean lips" (v. 5) has become for the time being unbridgeable. But—and Isaiah's commission attests to this—God remains in contact with humanity and does not give up on it. Vocations are a sign of hope. As long as God sends human beings, the world is not lost.

At the same time, moreover, this strange mission leaves Isaiah free of any compulsion to produce results or to succeed. Prophets and others called by God are often more familiar with resistance and obduracy than with the acceptance of their message. The taking of a clear stand for God frequently intensifies a latent rejection of his rule or lays bare an already existing rupture. In such situations, the coming of God's messengers provokes rejection and a turning away by the addressees. Those called have experienced this down to the present time. For this reason, Isaiah's mission can be a relief to them. What counts in God's eyes is not success but effort. The fruitfulness of a mission is up to God, and quite often the image of the grain of wheat (Jn 12:24) applies to it. Through the "death" of its rejection, God's word secures a new and stronger life later on.

In all this there is perhaps also a correction of traditional images of God. The passage says that he is incomparable in the heavenly sphere and among those who are his "equals" (vv. 2f.). In an unusually solemn setting, God also refuses to be limited to worship in the temple (vv. 1, 4) and rejects every attempt to limit him to a people or a country (v. 5: "the whole earth is full") and the usual conceptions of him. God's sending of human beings has salvation as its immediate and direct consequence (vv. 9f.). But even here the true God transcends all human thinking and, as a broad view shows, achieves his purposes even through suffering and hardship. The fact that this infinitely exalted king of the universe looks for willing human beings and asks for their help in his mission shows that he takes human freedom seriously and prefers to win it rather than force it.

QUESTIONS FOR REFLECTION

How alive in me is God as the Holy One who fills the universe and at the same time cautiously makes requests?

Was the experience of my own guilt ("unclean lips") and its forgiveness bestowed on me in connection with my mission?

"Send me!" Do I bring these words to my lips (in entreaty)? Is my offering of myself unlimited?

In my mission am I dependent on recognition and acceptance by others?

Can I endure failure, rejection? How do I deal with these?

7

A Pot Boils Over
Jeremiah, Prophet to the Nations—
City, Pillar, and Wall

Jeremiah 1

A pot boiling over causes panic at the stove. In the book of Jeremiah this image stands for the disaster that threatens to descend upon the community. Such situations call for human beings who are authentic and can bring help. Both of these apply to the prophet Jeremiah. His mission is not something added or learned; from the very beginning, even before his conception, God has prepared him for this task. And to a community whose most important buildings and with them a way of life have been destroyed, Jeremiah gives a new direction and security by his steadfastness and capacity for suffering. Jeremiah's vocation encourages others to trust, even in difficult situations, in the God who has always intimately known and interiorly strengthened those whom he calls.

Situation

A time of radical change—this is no doubt the correct description of the years during which the prophet Jeremiah made his appearance. The data in the introduction, that is, the brief facts given as a kind of heading to his book (Jer 1:1–3), show an activity covering exactly forty years. The thirteenth year of Josiah (1:2) corresponded to approximately 627 B.C., and the capture of Jerusalem (1:3) occurred in 587. It is hardly possible to gauge the extent of the changes that took place during those years.

In the eighteenth year of his reign (ca. 622) Josiah implemented the reform named after him (2 Kgs 22f.). It introduced a new religious discipline in many areas. The temple in Jerusalem became the only place in which the sacrifice of slaughtered animals could be offered. The other places of worship were eliminated, to some extent even destroyed. If their priests were worshipers of Yahweh, they could have a secondary position in Jerusalem. The priests of alien cults, however, were expelled or killed. The heart of the reform was a new consciousness of Yahweh as the only God and the God with whom the people were joined by a covenant—a concept that reflects the texts of Deuteronomy, which for this reason is regarded as having triggered this reform. Even if the reform of Josiah is a telescopic description that combines into a single happening events that took place over a longer period of time, it can nevertheless be compared with the extensive new order of things to which the Council of Trent, for example, or the Second Vatican Council gave the impulse.

There were still other changes in the political sphere. Josiah "the Good" was followed by relatively weak, dependent rulers, his sons Jehoiakim and Zedekiah, whose attention was directed abroad. Under the partial influence of the pro-Egyptian party in Judah, these two kings misjudged the changed world situation that had resulted from the battle of Carchemish and that favored the rising new Babylonian kingdom under Nebuchadnezzar. Rebellions against the supremacy of Babylon were promptly answered on each occasion by the siege of Jerusalem in 597 and again in 588/587, with this second siege leading to complete destruction of the city. This brought other great losses with it. In addition to the many deaths at the capture of the city, there was the loss of vitality due to the carrying off of so many into exile. The Davidic monarchy was forever ended.

It was into such a period of radical change that Jeremiah was sent. Jeremiah 1:1 tells us his name, "May God raise up!" and the name of his father, Hilkiah. Jeremiah came from the priestly ranks (the priesthood was at that time inherited) of the little Benjaminite tribe in Anatoth, a locality a few kilometers northeast of Jerusalem. Jeremiah is not the eternally complaining, incorrigible pessimist whom many people think him to be because of the passages in which he reproaches and accuses. He is, rather, the diagnostician of this radical change, analyzing the causes of the decline and pointing out ways for the future, a man full of hope in the God who embraces the whole of history and all peoples.

Structure

After the introduction the word-event formula, "And the word of the Lord came..." (v. 4), marks the beginning of our passage. At the same time, it marks the beginning of its first unit, Jeremiah's appointment as prophet to the nations (1:4–10). This appointment follows, in essentials, the call pattern familiar to us from the mission of Moses in Exodus 3 (v. 5: commission; v. 6: objection; v. 8: assurance; v. 9: sign).

Two word-event formulas (1:11, 13) divide the middle section (1:11–16). Each introduces a vision and its interpretation.

The emphatic address, "But you," in 1:17 marks the transition to the final section, which contains the concluding challenge and confirmation of Jeremiah's mission (1:17–19). This section is connected by its content with 1:4–10 (command to speak, theme of fear, God's promise).

Interpretation

The words "to me" in 1:4 make the prophet's experience available to his hearers. They are to share in the divine revelation given to him. Verse 5 describes God's activity as a movement that begins before Jeremiah's conception in his mother's womb (compare Paul, Gal 1:15) and leads, by way of "knowing" and "consecrating," to his prophetic task. In Jeremiah's case, the mission is not added on, as it were, to the rest of his life, as though it were something external. It is God's plan for him from the very outset, and it determines his entire existence. Jeremiah is a prophet to the nations; without this task he would not be Jeremiah. His mission is not simply a role, a piece of work, a duty; it is coextensive with his person and forms his identity. It is his deepest destiny and, at the same time, the expression of a special closeness ("know," "consecrate") to the one who creates and chooses him.

Jeremiah's first word, *ahah,* "Ah," in verse 6, provides a striking foretaste of his subsequent destiny that is so marked by lamentation and also introduces his objection. He thinks that he does not possess an essential ability ("speak") and that because of his youth he has no authority. In view of his quite extraordinary oratorical gifts (one need only read his texts), this objection must, as in the case of Moses, be understood as a subjective conviction of his inability and as completely at odds with his actual powers. Many who are called experience, especially during the early years, this conflict between the authority that is theirs by reason of their mission and their youthfulness, which is made perceptible by their as yet incomplete formation and their lack of experience. But if a person is ready to learn from others, the authority he has from his mission will be increasingly matched by his human maturity. Ideally, the two go together.

In a manner that seems hard, but is appropriate to the situation, God responds in verses 7–8 with commands. He refutes the objection of being too young with a reference to his own authority as sender; the second part of his answer (from "whatever I command you") cites Deuteronomy 18:18 and thus identifies Jeremiah as the prophet whom Moses had announced as one like himself. For this reason, and because of the promise of divine assistance, Jeremiah need not be afraid.

Verse 9 describes a powerful gesture. God stretches out his hand and touches the prophet's mouth. As compared with Isaiah 6:6–7, the gesture of touching is here much more direct. It confirms in a symbolic way the divine origin of Jeremiah's prophetic speech (again with a citation from Dt 18:18). In verse 10 Jeremiah is even appointed God's representative with universal authority (compare Jer 40:11 as the closest parallel to "I appoint you"). This is underscored by the series of verbs ("pluck up and pull down, destroy and overthrow, build and plant"), which are used elsewhere only of God. As human beings touched by God, those who are called can represent him to humanity. Their speech obtains a hearing for God.

In verses 11–16 Jeremiah is given a new way of seeing things. Twice God takes things seen every day and interprets them in plays on words that yield a deeper meaning. In verse 11 the almond branch (which in Hebrew is also called "watcher," because it blooms early) is an image of God's alert attention to the fulfillment of his word (v. 12; similarly, Is 55:11). The pot boiling over in verse 13 gives advance notice of the judgment descending on Judah and Jerusalem (vv. 14f.). The two visions together form the *basso continuo* for Jeremiah's activity: amid all the disaster and collapse, God remains the watcher. Jeremiah 31:28 will later turn this image completely to the good.

As though preparing for toil or battle, Jeremiah is now to gather up his long robe (v. 17) and proceed without worry to his work of proclamation. The demand that he not be afraid points once again to the divine origin of his mission. Those whom God takes into his service should not be afraid of human beings; otherwise they betray their mission and are left to their crippling insecurity and fearfulness. Jesus will later encourage his disciples along the same lines (Mk 13:9ff.).

To a modern reader the descriptions in verse 18 will probably sound odd. As Jeremiah was made a prophet to the nations in verse 5, so here he is made "a fortified city, an iron pillar, and a bronze wall." Extending the image of the protection given to him against the hostility of those in authority over the people, Jeremiah takes on the role of a replacement for what is being lost. Since the capital and the temple are to be destroyed, he receives their function (the Hebrew preposition has two meanings, "against" and "for") of supporting both authorities and people through the transition. Those who listen to him find in him a city and walls in place of Jerusalem, that is, community and security, and instead of the temple with its bronze columns that have been carried away (see 5:17ff.), a firmer ("iron"), more lasting showpiece as their access to God. Those called become the support, protection, and ornament of a community that heeds them.

But Jeremiah still has battles to face (v. 19). He can face them with the promise of God's help repeated from verse 8. With this he is unconquerable.

Perspectives

The gnawing question of whether God's call turns a young man or woman into something alien to him or her is answered in Jeremiah 1. God's mission is the very essence of a person. Those called do not thereby lose their identity. On the contrary, it is only in the carrying out of this commission that they do justice to their innermost selves. It is a consoling and strengthening thing to know that one's entire life is so embraced by God. In the case of Jeremiah, this being grounded in God, beginning even before his bodily existence, is the foundation that enables him to cope with his hard destiny.

A comparison between the person of the prophet and the tasks laid on him reveals a sharp contrast. Jeremiah's despondent complaint, his conviction of being unfit, and his youth contrast with the divine authorization. This last singles him out not only as a prophet in the line of Moses, but also as one who has a mission to the nations (that is, not to Judah alone), as a universal representative of God, and, finally, as a superior replacement for the city being destroyed and for its temple. Such a disproportion between the individual's abilities and the qualification given him by God is to be seen in many who are called. Every vocation embodies a paradox in which God shines forth.

Unwearyingly and powerfully, God calls upon Jeremiah to

be fearless. The support of God's commission makes it possible to work on one's own timidity and to overcome it. As a result, when external securities (city, temple) disappear, those called, together with their message, become a new and better foundation for believers.

QUESTIONS FOR REFLECTION

God chooses Jeremiah even before his conception. To what extent do my mission and my identity go together? Is my call coextensive with my person? Or am I playing a part that has little to do with my real self?

The call to be a "prophet to the nations" sets aside narrow national boundaries. Do we likewise understand ourselves to be universal representatives of God, with a mission to the whole of humankind? Or do we serve predominantly the interests of small groups?

God forbids Jeremiah to be afraid and promises him his assistance. When have God or other human beings helped me to overcome my fears? Have I the courage to confess my vocation even publicly and, as a result, to endure conflicts?

8

Overcome by the Glory of Yahweh
Ezekiel Is Sent to a "Rebellious House"

Ezekiel 1—3

*C*ountless human beings are in flight today or must remain permanently in distant lands. Ezekiel's call is a source of hope for them. It describes a God who does not abandon his people in their exile and a prophet who is wholly at God's disposal. With Ezekiel as his agent, God shows human beings in exile new paths to life. The point of departure for this call is the extremely fascinating manifestation of this God's glory, which is both an answer to the haunting questions of exiled humanity and an unforgettable depiction of the fullness of the divine life.

Situation

The first siege and capture of Jerusalem by the Babylonians in 597 B.C. was a shock (2 Kgs 24:8–17). Yahweh, the God of Israel, had not preserved Judah; its capital, Jerusalem; and, above all, his own temple, from humiliation by enemies of a different faith. In addition, thousands had to go into exile in Mesopotamia, Ezekiel the priest among them.

Ezekiel 1 mentions the "river Chebar" (1:1), a canal that branched off from the Euphrates at Babylon. Beside it lay one of the settlements in which the Babylonians allowed the deportees (*gola* = "a leading away," "those led away") to live together. It was named Tel-abib (3:15; Hebrew: "Hill of the Ears [of grain]"), hence the name of the present Tel Aviv in Israel; but originally it was probably the Akkadian *til-abubi,* "Hill of the Flood." While the lot of these displaced people was better than that of the people of the northern kingdom, Israel, whom the Assyrians scattered far and wide in 722 B.C., they still had a difficult time of it. They had to live without their accustomed community, without their own lands, without their familiar work, and, at the same time, with the memory of a humiliating defeat. Their uprooting was made worse by the contemporary conception of "foreign parts." In their view, distant lands were unclean (Am 7:17), the domain of other gods, who could demand worship from them.

In addition, the culture and religion of the conqueror's country exerted a constant pressure toward interbreeding. The spiritual foundations of the exile were called into question by the sumptuous magnificence of Babylon, the capital, with its efficient organization, its seemingly unconquerable military might, and its splendid processions and temples. In comparison, the homeland of the exiles must have seemed absolutely pathetic. These experiences were a challenge to their faith in God. Questions arose: Can our God, Yahweh, hold his own against these other, victorious gods? Is Yahweh, to whom we prayed back home, also present and relevant here in this distant land? Is the divine, in the final analysis, a brutal, "bestial" power, as experienced in our ruin, or does it have a "human" face? At the deepest level: Does God bring destruction or an encounter marked by understanding? Ezekiel 1 answers these questions.

Structure

The call of Ezekiel, which extends over three chapters, is the most detailed one in the Bible. To this detail the very lengthy setting of the scene and the divine manifestation in chapter 1 contribute substantially. This ample presentation reflects the weight that the biblical narrator assigns to the introductory vision of God. The vision of God is the supporting basis for the mission that follows

(Ez 2f.). Vision and mission together are the foundation of the prophetic message and the book.

The overwhelming vision of God in Ezekiel 1 is given its structure by the phrase "(and) I saw" (NRSV: "as I looked"), which is repeated six times:

> in 1:1 for the title, vv. 1–3;
> in 1:4 as introduction to the first main section, vv. 4–14;
> in 1:15, introducing the second main section vv. 15–26;
> in the culminating conclusion, 1:27f., three times.

The call proper then follows in a concentric arrangement:

> 2.1f. The spirit sets me on my feet (a)
>   vv. 3–5. Mission (b)
>   vv. 6f. Fearlessness amid resistance of the people (c)
>   vv. 8–10. Giving of the scroll (d)
>   3:1–3. Eating of the scroll (d')
>   vv. 4–9. Preparation of Ezekiel to meet resistance (c')
>   vv. 10f. Invitation to begin the mission (b')
> vv. 12–15. The spirit lifted me up (a')

The center of this circular composition is the events connected with the scroll (d-d'). The obedient "eating" of the scroll contrasts with the opposition of the people to God. To describe this the characteristic word *meri,* "rebelliousness," is used eight times in Ezekiel 2 and following. This rejection explains the adjacent sections on the fearlessness and preparation of Ezekiel (c-c') without which he cannot carry out his mission (b-b'). With him goes the supporting action of the spirit, who at the beginning (a), after the moving vision, turns him into an upright hearer of God. The spirit also helps him on his way to his mission, back into the community (a').

Two additions are thematically connected with all this and follow upon it, even though they are separated by a period of seven days (3:15f.). In 3:16–21 God communicates to the prophet the role of a sentinel, whose task is to give warning (on this point see also Ez 18 and 33:1–20). Ezekiel 3:22–27 describes the muteness ordered by God as a counterweight. On the one hand, these last verses hark back repeatedly to the call of Ezekiel ("the glory of Yahweh," "fall down," "being set on his feet," "open the mouth"). On the other, due to the prophetic symbolic action and the place where this happens, namely, "the valley," these verses also prepare the way for future passages (e.g., Ez 4 or 37, the awakening of the dead bones).

Even though Ezekiel's call is described at great length, he himself does not say a word. The call is a happening that lays hold of him and overpowers him (see his falling on his face in 1:28 and his standing up due to the power of another in 2:2). He is not a partner in a dialogue with God, but a recipient of God's word through hearing and complete interiorizing ("eat," 3:2). Ezekiel's passive, receptive behavior reflects another essential trait of vocations: they can never be initiated by human beings, no matter how hard someone may try. A vocation always remains a claim from outside to which those called open themselves.

Ezekiel's complete readiness to serve and the contrast between this and the rebellious house mean that the call pattern familiar from most of the other stories is not applied here. For even if Israel rebels a thousand times against God, at least one man, Ezekiel, has not uttered even a single objection against him. As a result, there is no place for the elements of "assurance" and "sign," although the manifestation of God's glory in Ezekiel 1 more than compensates for the latter. (The same can be said for the much more modest vision in Is 6.) And instead of the element of "distress," we find a deeper suffering, which consists in the people's rejection of God and the hardening of their hearts against him.

Finally, reference should be made to the formula "whether they hear or refuse to hear," which is typical of Ezekiel 2—3 (see 2:5, 7; 3:11; and, in an alternate form, 3:27). This formula serves to conclude smaller units and to declare a twofold freedom: the prophet is free from every compulsion to achieve success, and his addressees are likewise free to accept the message. Despite their rejection (mentioned over 30 times in Ez 2f.), God offers it to them through Ezekiel.

Interpretation

The Manifestation of Yahweh's Glory (Ez 1)

The seemingly discordant dates given in 1:1–2 are probably to be understood thus: the "thirtieth year" in verse 1 gives Ezekiel's age, while the "fifth year" in verse 2 refers to King Jehoiachin, who was carried off in 597 B.C. The fifth day in the fourth month of his fifth year refers, therefore, with high probability, to a day in July 593. Being in his thirtieth year, Ezekiel could already have entered upon his service as priest in the temple (Nm 4:3), but this is now impossible for him as an exile. God calls him instead to service as a prophet. What he misses at home is given to him in abundance in a distant land. The opening three verses are full of allusions to the divine revelation bestowed on Ezekiel: the opening of the heavens, the vision of God, the word and hand of Yahweh.

Verse 4 introduces the first section of the vision (vv. 4–14; see Structure) with the phrase "As I looked." Referring as it does to wind, storm, cloud, fire, and shining, the section contains, tightly packed together, an abundance of the elements connected with manifestations of God (e.g., Ps 18:9–13; Job 38:1; Ex 13:21f.). But at this point Ezekiel's gaze falls upon four strange living creatures. Although these have bestial superhuman powers—calves' feet; wings; faces of ox, lion, and eagle (vv. 7–11)—their dominant element is the human. They resemble human beings (v. 5), they have human hands (v. 8), and the primary face, which is evidently turned to the front, is a human face (v. 10). Along with their humanity, their mobility is especially emphasized: they can go straight ahead in all four directions (this is connected with the fact that they are four in number) without turning.

The next "As I looked," in verse 15, introduces the second section (vv. 15–26) and heightens the element of mobility even further through the image of the wheels, which support a "firmament" (v. 22) like the firmament of the heavens (Gn 1:6) with a throne like sapphire above it (v. 26; compare the encounter with God in Ex 24:10). The entire manifestation is accompanied by mighty thunder (v. 24) and reaches its climax in the description of the one who sits on the throne and resembles a human being (v. 26).

Verses 27–28 conclude the entire vision with a threefold "And I saw." To the elements of the divine manifestation already mentioned in verse 4 is added the (rain) "bow" (v. 28; see Gn 9:13). Ezekiel very cautiously describes this manifestation as "the appearance of the likeness of the glory of Yahweh" (v. 28). This description safeguards the transcendence of God by means of three limiting mediations. The vision does not communicate Yahweh himself, but is only (1) the appearance (2) of the likeness (3) of his glory. Even that is enough to make Ezekiel fall to the ground.

According to the testimony of the first creation story, the human being is created in the image and likeness of God (Gn 1:26). Ezekiel 1:26 constitutes a complementary statement: if God is to be compared with anything at all, the human being is the most likely reality ("something that seemed like a human form," v. 26, formulated with the same kind of cautiousness as in v. 28). This once again repeats the emphasis on human features that we already saw in the four living creatures. Yahweh's glory manifests itself not in the violence of the elements of nature, not in the unrestrained power of the beasts, not in the force of the thundering noises, but in that he is, in his likeness, closest to human beings. Israel, Ezekiel, and all of humanity may trust that God is close to them. Just as they are created in his image, so Yahweh has a "human face." He is not a demon who acts arbitrarily.

Those who have been carried off must have been asking

themselves whether their God had remained back home in Palestine. The effortless motion of the living creatures and the wheels makes it clear that God, with his spirit/wind (1:12, 20), is not confined to any place but shows his radiant power both at home and in a distant land. God's "glory" abandons even the temple of Jerusalem because of the atrocities that have taken place there (Ez 9:3; 10:18f.; 11:22f.) and has gone eastward, in the direction of the exiles. Together with those dragged off, Ezekiel and all who are called may experience that God is everywhere.

To go as one sent by God often means abandoning one's homeland and sometimes having, like Jesus, no place to stay (Lk 9:58). In addition, a call is usually accompanied by a series of moves. To one who thus "leaves houses and fields" (Mt 19:29) in his service, God will show himself even more gloriously in a distant land.

A further urgent question in exile was whether Yahweh could hold his own amid the splendor of the Babylonian gods and their great statues, temples, and processions. Ezekiel 1 describes Yahweh's manifestation as utterly fascinating. Natural elements, beings never seen before, radiant light, and precious metals and stones combine with movement and a powerful background of noise to form a manifestation that in its magnificence leaves far behind anything hitherto experienced. At the same time, all these aspects merge with one another to such a degree that despite the detailed description, the whole is difficult to grasp. This means that the glory of Yahweh is in itself more fascinating than human beings can imagine. How much more fascinating, then, is Yahweh himself! Part of a vocation is to be gripped, as Ezekiel was, by the radiance of God.

Ezekiel's Mission (Ez 2:1—3:15)

Even though his messenger is only a "mortal" or a "creature," God wants to look him in the face as he commissions him (2:1). If this messenger is unable to stand up straight, the Spirit comes to his aid (v. 2). Ezekiel may stand before him as a trusted servant before his master (see Dt 1:38 for Joshua; 1 Kgs 10:8 for Solomon's ministers).

So personal a relationship can sustain even a difficult mission (v. 3). Ezekiel is being sent to the Israelites, who are described as "rebellious nations," a phrase that occurs only here in the plural (the reference is probably to the groups of Israelites dispersed through the various countries of the Near East) and as being from time immemorial ("their ancestors") hardened in sinfulness. To their children, who are the equals of their fathers when it comes to pigheadedness (literally, "tough faced") and hardness of heart, Ezekiel must prove himself to be God's messenger: "Thus says the Lord Yahweh." It does not matter to him whether they accept or reject him; it is enough that they know him to be a prophet, a speaker who comes from God (v. 5; also 33:33). God will not force them to accept his message but wants at least to ensure that they hear him.

The task of God's messengers is to present people with God's word, whether or not the time is favorable (2 Tm 4:2). The fear that surfaces in the prophet is met by God with the threefold urging: "Do not be afraid" (v. 6). Even if, as the text says literally, they "are rebellious and thorns [turned] against you, and you sit on scorpions," Ezekiel is to be undismayed and to proclaim God's message ("my words," v. 7, in contrast to "their words," twice in v. 6). The image, used only here in the Bible, of sitting on stinging, poisonous insects, makes graphically clear the hostility he will meet. In the passion of Jesus and in the fate of countless persons called, this picturesque language has become cruel reality.

God hopes to find in Ezekiel an obedient recipient of his message. The opening of the mouth and the eating (v. 8) signify an eager and complete acceptance and turn the prophet into a person who is the opposite of the rebellious people. This kind of interiorization extends in principle to everything that God proffers. Not until verse 9 is the eating of the scroll made concrete; it is extended to Ezekiel by God's hand. In Jeremiah 1:9 God communicates his word by touching with his hand; here the divine word has already become a "book," thus pointing to an advanced stage of prophetic proclamation. Unlike speech, writing remains; God's word becomes a message that reaches beyond the present moment. The message is presented to Ezekiel and is full of lamentation (v. 10).

The renewed command to eat (3:1) clarifies the meaning. The interior acceptance of God's word is a condition for the mission (the key word is "Go!") and the preaching. In verse 2 Ezekiel's openness is linked to a feeding by God, as though he were a little child. He must really swallow what is given to him (v. 3) so that it reaches "stomach and insides," the place where babies grow and where the center of the human being is. But already in his mouth the (bitter) lamentations turn into sweetness: there is a transforming power hidden in obedient acceptance. In this phenomenon the paradoxical character of the divine being itself shines through (see comments above on Ex 3:2).

Every life demands a great deal of swallowing. Many relationships are disordered but cannot be changed. The idiosyncrasies of our fellow human beings bother us, but we cannot improve them. Decisions made by others require us to get involved in something new or to endure a dependence. Now if human beings can demand such readiness of us, all the more can the true God, who is concerned with the salvation of humanity. The point, however, is not just to swallow everything, but rather to cultivate a basic availability that counteracts the illusion of complete self-determination. Those who consent to this availability may experience that a swallowing that initially caused revulsion can turn into the ingestion of a strengthening nourishment that enlivens us and makes us strong. This is the meaning of Jesus' statement that his food is to do the Father's will (Jn 4:34). Ezekiel is a model for all those who willingly accept what befalls them. Through their yes to God's challenge, those who are called live in solidarity with the millions of human beings who accept far heavier demands without ever having a chance to improve their painful lot.

Along with his demand for proclamation (v. 4), God again makes clear the difficulty of the mission. A foreign people, speaking an alien, incomprehensible language (v. 5f.; literally, "of deep lips and heavy tongue"; see Ex 4:10) would listen even if God were not (thus the Hebrew text) to send Ezekiel to them. Israel, on the contrary, will not listen to the prophets any more than to God (v. 7). The rejection of God that comes from a hardening of face and heart (as in 2:4) applies in equal measure to those whom he calls (as with Jesus; see Jn 15:20). Those called enter into a common fate with God. They cannot expect to be treated better than he is. But at the same time they are already sharing in his fullness of life.

Ezekiel is now armed against the resistance of the people (v. 8f.). Not his heart, but his face and brow are hardened so that he will be able to stand up to them. The comparison with a diamond signifies an unconquerable strength that need fear nothing. Action on behalf of God calls for steadfastness. Even today this attitude is required of those called. The way to salvation passes through self-surrender, honesty, and sympathetic love. Those called have the responsibility of pointing human beings away from their tendencies to selfishness, dishonesty, and hatred and toward the way that truly leads to their happiness. The hardness in question is not a self-centered stubbornness but a strength given by God for meeting resistance. Despite all their weaknesses, those called go forward in the purity of their mission. In the same way Jesus sends disciples "like sheep into the midst of wolves" (Mt 10:16).

God concludes by repeating important themes of the mission (vv. 10f.). Ezekiel's own interior acceptance of God's words with heart and ears is the basis for his being able to repeat the message. His mission affects the *gola,* the exiles (this is something new, v. 11). Ezekiel must show himself to them as God's messenger, independently of their reaction.

The burden imposed by this task does not permit any undertaking by one's own power. It is only as one carried by the spirit of

God (twice, vv. 12 and 14) that Ezekiel is able to undertake the execution of his task. In addition to the elements already named in Ezekiel 1, the appearance of God concludes with the rumbling of an earthquake (compare 1 Kgs 19:11) and is accompanied by a solemn proclamation: "Blessed be the glory of God from its place!" (v. 12b., literal translation instead of "the glory of God rose from its place"). All calls allow God's being to shine out more clearly. It is only fitting that they be followed by blessing and praise. Today too, those called are often filled with jubilant praise and gratitude.

But Ezekiel's mission also awakens bitterness, distress, and "excitement of spirit" (v. 14). To be sent by God transforms a person. It leaves those called different from what they were before. Those affected feel as though they were seized and gripped by a mighty power (the "hand" of Yahweh, as earlier in 1:3; 2:9). And this condition continues after the return to everyday life and to the community (v. 15). Ezekiel remains troubled and dazed for "seven days," that is, for a somewhat lengthy, complete, and rounded period, among his own people. Ezekiel 3:12 and 14–15 accurately describe the alternation of emotions in those called. Rejoicing in God and deep consternation follow upon one another, often with no connection between them.

The divine commission has made Ezekiel a different person, and God allows him a period to reorient himself. During that time the prophet is able slowly to assimilate the change that has taken place in him. After that, God speaks to him again (3:16ff.) and enables him to begin his mission in concrete form (3:22ff. as transition to 4:1ff.).

Perspectives

Ezekiel 1—3 lays the groundwork for Ezekiel's activity. His message of judgment (Ez 4ff.) but also his experience of the "mobile" glory of God (9:3; 10:18f.) are already to be seen here from the very beginning. The encounter with God at the beginning of his vocation is the root out of which the future develops, including the salvation that comes increasingly to the fore from Ezekiel 34 on.

Ezekiel's call springs from the situation of the Exile. The distress experienced in a distant land and the destruction of ideas and relationships that had been taken for granted had profoundly unsettled people. If in this situation God communicates with one of their number and entrusts him with a mission, this means that despite everything he is not giving up on them. Ezekiel's mission thus becomes a sign to his fellow countrymen that God still intends to journey with them. Despite their rejection of him, God is giving them a new chance.

Ezekiel's actual commissioning is not accompanied by any content. Apart from the formula proper to a messenger, "Thus says the Lord Yahweh" (2:4; 3:11), which is the proof that he is one sent, there is no mention of a message to be delivered. Ezekiel accepts a task, the substance of which even he himself does not know. What is to sustain him is not so much the knowledge of a program but, on the one hand, the encounter he experiences here with the God who is mighty even in a foreign land, and on the other, his own complete openness to the words of this God.

The constant description of the prophet as "child of man" (from 2:1 on) brings out even more strongly the contrast with the tremendous vision in Ezekiel 1. While the human being as such is always a child, one conceived and born of others, one naturally dependent and small, here the human being disappears almost completely in comparison with the glory of Yahweh. Yet God is interested in this human being and appoints him to be his messenger.

Ezekiel appears here to be weak. He is hardly capable of movement; he is completely overwhelmed by what is happening and does not utter a word. It is God's elective will and not any deep piety, special gifts, or other human merits that constitutes a vocation. God not only sends but also prepares those whom he calls for their tasks. In the process, personal traits (e.g., Ezekiel's consternation, 3:14f.) are combined with characteristics received from God ("hard face," 3:8). In those who are called, the self and grace flourish in a wonderful symbiosis.

QUESTIONS FOR REFLECTION

Ezekiel is completely engulfed by the glory of Yahweh. Does God fascinate us? How has he shown himself to us?

To eat the scroll means to absorb God's word interiorly. How deeply has that word taken root in us?

Despite his hard brow and face, Ezekiel is deeply affected interiorly. Are the two things, strength and sympathy, also present in us? Or do we tend in only one direction?

Ezekiel's mission has no "program," no content. In the midst of that kind of uncertainty, am I sustained by my relationship with God so as to persevere in living my mission?

9

The Concert of Voices
Consolation from the Herald of Joy

Isaiah 40:1–11

Why go on believing when almost everything has collapsed? Why go on living when grief and loss have become almost intolerable? "Because God himself is coming" is the answer given to these questions by Second Isaiah at the beginning of his prophecy. To announce this coming and to prepare for it was the task of several individuals. Their vocation can be a model even for our day because it counteracts crippling resignation with the divine message of joyous hope in the future and of a new community.

Situation

The capture of Jerusalem in 587 B.C. by the troops of the Babylonian King Nebuchadnezzar had far-reaching consequences. All that had hitherto sustained the people in the southern kingdom of Judah was destroyed or called into question. For hundreds of years to come they had lost their political independence. The destruction of the capital, Jerusalem, was a blow from which not only the city itself but the entire region would not recover for many decades. The social and economic situation remained desperate. A large part of the upper class had been led off into exile in Babylon. These events and other causes led to indescribable suffering among the people in Judah. The temple lay in ruins, desecrated, and the faithful were forced to ask what Yahweh, their God, was doing and why he had permitted such a defeat. This unhappy, oppressive state of affairs is reflected in many texts of the Bible, for example, Lamentations, Psalm 137, and other texts.

And yet, forty-eight years later something happened far from Jerusalem that was to have major repercussions throughout the entire Near East for a long time to come. Cyrus, the Persian king, entered Babylon and put an end to the rule of the Babylonians. Thus began the era of the Persian Empire marked by greater respect for individuals, including defeated peoples and their religions. As a result of this tolerance, the Jews received permission to return to their country and even to rebuild the temple (probably under Darius I in the years 520–15).

Even though the page of history was beginning to turn at the level of the general political climate, conditions in Judah remained difficult for a long time. A great deal of the country had to be built up and reorganized in the face of much opposition. It is to this situation that the texts of Second Isaiah are addressed. Their hopeful, encouraging message has made them part of the imperishable treasure of the Bible.

Structure

Isaiah 36—39 speaks of the threat to Jerusalem from the Assyrian siege of 701 B.C., but the real background is the Babylonian attack in 588/7. This threat, which has meanwhile become a painful reality, is the correct reference point of the texts of Second Isaiah (Is 40—55) with their vision of a change in fortunes. Isaiah 40:1–11 begins these texts and is to be regarded as a prologue or overture to them. For these verses contain a short collection of important key words and themes of Second Isaiah.

The numerous admonitions to speak aloud make it possible to see in Isaiah 40:1–11 a series of calls that start with God (vv. 1f.) and reach to the herald of good tidings (v. 9). The herald is to communicate to the cities of Judah the joyous news of God's coming. What is unique in all this is that God's order is transmitted by a number of speakers. There is, as it were, a small sacred concert with different voices. In verses 1–2 the speaker is God; in verses 3–5, the voice that cries; in verses 6–8, the voice that speaks and the speaker of the words "What shall I cry?" (the preceding words in verse 6 should be translated "and someone says," not "and I said"!); in verses 9–11, the giver of the order to the herald of joy. No other passage of the Old Testament shows so beautifully how a commission does not arise simply out of a close togetherness with God of the one called, but also needs other human beings and their cooperation. Today, too, those called are not meant to be isolated, snobbish virtuosos. They play in harmony with many others and only together produce the sound of God's music.

Many readers may find it surprising to see Isaiah 40 placed in the category of calls. The key words *go* and *send* do not appear; everything is shifted to the level of speaking, to do which the herald of joy must climb a high mountain (v. 9). Nevertheless, our text as a whole does follow the now-familiar call pattern.

The reference to a distress can be seen in verses 1–2, where guilt and sin are mentioned, and the call to comfort presupposes suffering and sorrow. The element of commissioning is found frequently: from verse 1 to the beginning of verse 6 there are numerous commands. The command "Cry out!" in verse 6 meets with an objection from an unidentified individual: "What shall I cry? All flesh (after all) is grass…for Yahweh's breath blows upon it." Taking up this objection, the voice—probably the one mentioned at the beginning of verse 6—begins to speak again in the last sentence of verse 7: "Surely, the people are grass…but the word of our God persists for ever." The everlastingness of the divine word in verse 8 can be understood as a kind of assurance, just as in verses 9–11 the coming of God can be taken in a vague sense as a sign, even though the classical expression "I will be with you" or the word *sign* are admittedly absent.

Although many components of the call pattern take a different form, Isaiah 40:1–11 as a whole does therefore contain echoes of the call pattern. In addition, its position at the beginning of

Second Isaiah is a point in favor of its interpretation as a call. In it, several persons are commissioned to proclaim aloud the joyous message of God's coming as a response to a resigned vision of human transiency. When human beings accept the fact that they are frail and that God has allowed destruction, then the liberating tidings of God's recent turning back to them can strike deep roots. On the other hand, human beings who regard themselves as upright and strong, or who are determined to do everything on their own and in complete independence, do not listen to such a message. But their need of redemption is all the more pressing.

Interpretation

The twofold imperative "Comfort! Comfort!" in verse 1 represents a very urgent command (see Is 51:9, 17; 52:1, 11; etc., for the same device with other verbs). The parallel phrase "Speak to the heart" in verse 2 (literally: "against the heart" = to speak against false [opposite] attitudes of the heart) contains this element of comfort, along with encouragement (Hos 2:14; Gn 34:3). God wants others (he is addressing a plurality) to give the city of Jerusalem new encouragement in its grief. He gives several reasons for this hope. The end of its forced labor, the payment of its debt, its double suffering (probably in accordance with the decree in Ex 22:7 that whoever misappropriates the possessions of another must replace it with twice as much) are images showing that it has finished its painful time of penance for its earlier transgressions. The realization that the burden of guilt has been discharged opens the way to new life.

Immediately in verse 3, the first speaker begins the proclamation. In a loud voice the speaker orders the building of a highway for Yahweh: a raised road that is comfortable to use (in a modern setting, a promenade). On this road, which passes through the wilderness of disappointment, despair, and abandoned hope,

God is to find easy access to his faithful, who see themselves as a community ("our" God: the confession is that of a group). Five hundred years later, but with "wilderness" as a description of place, John the Baptist will address the same message to human beings (Mk 1:3). The unending task of those called is to prepare the way for God. All their labors have as their goal that God himself should find acceptance in humanity.

Four details in verse 4 continue the image of roadbuilding in verse 3 and interpret it. Everything that represents an obstacle is to be turned into a level road, not by means of bridges and tunnels as is done today, but by leveling the ground. Differences that separate are to be removed. In a transferred sense, people with a mistrust of life, an exaggerated need of recognition, wrong attitudes ("valley, mountain, crooked ground"; this last word contains the root of the name Jacob; see Gn 27:36) are to surrender their differences and meet on a common level. When this kind of common agreement overcomes the obstacles to God's coming, the glory of Yahweh shines out (v. 5). When those who believe in God deal with one another and live together in mutual love despite all their differences, this attests to the hidden action of God. Then all human beings will know that God himself has "spoken," that is, has given the command and the power to live in this way.

In verse 6 a second voice urges others to cry out, but it meets with objection from a third party. This third, unidentified speaker personifies the mood of resignation that is widespread among the people. In the face of the transiency that human beings experience in so many ways and so oppressively, and also of their lack of solidarity and constancy, everything else, even this proclamation, seems meaningless. This is all the more so since the "breath of the Lord"—which elsewhere is a life-giving, transforming, liberating force (Jgs 3:10; 11:29; Is 11:2; Ez 37)—here causes the people to wither.

In the last sentence of verse 7 the second speaker makes his presence known again and acknowledges that the objecting voice is correct: the radical changes and terrors of the past decades have shown how frail human beings are ("the people are grass") and that they pass away like other natural growths. The second speaker thus affirms the experience of the resigned people, but then, in his final statement at the end of verse 8, he sets alongside it, trenchantly and confidently, the everlastingness of the divine word. Those who focus on the turning wheel of human transiency can easily become discouraged. The second speaker contrasts with that the everlasting validity of the divine promises and therefore also of the message of comfort that is issued here. Those who are called share in God's breadth and eternity. He helps them direct the gaze of men and women beyond the moment so that they may look past their own fixations or blinders and recognize his plans at work in larger contexts. At the end of Second Isaiah (55:10f.) the divine word is once again the focus of attention: God himself watches over it to ensure that it is fruitful.

Such a message cannot be silenced. Verse 9 calls upon an unidentified female, to whom the honorific title "Herald of Joy" is given, to cry out, as loudly as she can and without any apprehensive restraint, to Zion/Jerusalem and the cities of Judah: "See, (here is) your God!" As on other occasions in the history of Israel, the proclamation of God's great deeds or saving victories is a task for women also (Ex 15:20f.; Jgs 5; 11:34; 1 Sm 18:6f.). The woman addressed here is likewise to take an ideal, lofty position for her call. In the expression of emotions, here of jubilation, women obviously have it easier. But there is more than this in the choice of a woman: after the destruction of Jerusalem, the part played by women emerges more clearly in the literature. This is in keeping with the greater esteem that is beginning to be given to them at that time. These are early footsteps on the road to the acknowledgment of the equality of the sexes.

Verses 10–11 repeat the content of the message of joy and depict the coming of Yahweh from two points of view, both of them connected with the image of the "arm." In its first occurrence, the "arm" is the embodiment of the strength that brings with it reward, acquisition. In its second occurrence, it represents the tender care that God the Shepherd shows to the little ones, the weak ones ("the lambs"). The text ends with this order to proclaim the coming of Yahweh, the strong, solicitous God.

Perspectives

Second Isaiah begins with a kind of "call." In this call, unlike others, several persons are asked to announce the incredible message of God's coming into a situation of distress. It is not an individual leader or prophet but several different persons from both sexes who together receive the task of proclaiming and preparing for this new coming of God.

The difficulty of their task can be perceived from the expressions used in verse 4 and the objection raised in verses 6–7. A crippling, oppressive atmosphere has been created by the differences and lack of authenticity among the people that have hitherto made genuine community impossible, as well as by the widespread hopelessness that makes the effort of calling seem in vain. It would be beyond the strength of any one individual to combat it, but God's commission is addressed to a plurality, to a group. There is a chance that in concert they can overcome the resignation of the people; bear witness to the consoling, encouraging, gloriously resplendent God; and arouse confidence in his word that stands forever.

The main task of this group is to make fearless proclamation in a loud and audible voice. They shall, as it were, advertise this "message of joy" that seems so difficult to accept. This Hebrew expression (the corresponding term in Greek and Latin is *evangelium,* "good news") occurs several times more in Second Isaiah (41:27 and 52:7; also 61:1). Even before God changes the situation, he makes this known to his people. As a result their hope is roused in advance, and they are able to recognize Yahweh as the one who not only announces salvation but also accomplishes it (e.g., in rich abundance at the end of Second Isaiah in 54—55).

In our day too, the proclamation is not simply a "job" for individualists. More than ever it calls for the teamwork of all whom God calls, without differentiation by age, race, sex, or strength of voice. In a world that talks of "no future" and is full of pessimistic and skeptical attitudes toward life, those who believe in the God of the Bible have as their task to proclaim the liberating coming and presence of this God who is well disposed precisely to those human beings who are suffering. Not only is such an announcement able to awaken hope and good cheer in its addressees, but it is also an honor and a joy for those making the proclamation.

QUESTIONS FOR REFLECTION

God's commission is given to many. To what extent does my life reflect this shared mission/vocation?

Do I dare to proclaim God's message of joy in the face of widespread hopelessness? Prominently, at the top of my voice, without fear?

God comes, consoling, gloriously strong, and protecting. Am I myself open and prepared for him?

10

Priestly Kingdom and Holy Nation
The Last Movement of the Old Testament

We have meditated rather closely on nine passages about call-ing from Moses to Second Isaiah. Yet this is far from having said everything. On the one hand, there is in the Old Testament a series of other passages referring to calls, and we want to touch on these by way of conclusion. On the other hand, the New Testament con-tinues this set of themes and gives them a wholly new (christolog-ical) accent when speaking of the following of Jesus.

Three fundamental and constant elements are found in every call: (a) God makes a demand of a human being whom he has chosen; (b) these individuals to whom God speaks combine a "passive" being-called with their own "active" readiness; and (c) their call is given not for their own sake but for the sake of a com-munity. In the first three objections that Moses raised in connec-tion with his call, we see the "you/he" of God who sends, the "I" of Moses, and the "they" of the people. We want now to look more closely at these aspects, beginning with the last.

Vocations are woven into the network that is the community (c). Moses receives his brother Aaron as his partner; Samuel learns from Eli, his teacher; and in Second Isaiah several persons receive the task of comforting. Others always play a part or are affected. The supporting network of the community can also be seen in the vocations of Joshua and Barak. In Joshua 1:16–18 the officers of the people assure Joshua of their full support and encourage him with God's own words: "Be strong and coura-geous" (see vv. 6f., 9). This reinforcement by those in positions of responsibility supports the person who succeeds an exceptional predecessor. Joshua, previously a servant, is now able to take over the burden of leadership from Moses, and this in a critical phase, that of the occupation of Canaan.

Judges 4 describes in an almost humorous way this quest of support for a mission. Barak, the leader of the Israelite tribes, is willing to undertake his task only along with a woman, Deborah the judge. "If you will go with me" is the condition he sets down (v. 8), alluding to the promise of support, which is the fourth element in the call pattern. This "courage" of the man finds its counterpart in the fact that the honors of victory will go to a woman (v. 9). As we saw in the story of Samson's mother (Jgs 13), so in Judges 4 the part played by a woman is emphasized. God's call to Barak is mediated by one of women's outstanding representatives, and both sexes work together for the liberation.

A community can be a supporting network for those who are called, but these in turn help to consolidate the network and give it a new form. This is made clear in the first passage of the Bible that speaks of a mission from God. In Genesis 45 Joseph makes himself known to the brothers who had sold him to traders going to Egypt, and he interprets this atrocious deed born of hatred by saying, "God sent me before you to preserve you" (vv. 5 and 7f.). A man who himself had to endure great suffering and injustice is able later on to see his lot as a mission from God and, by this conciliatory interpretation of it, to create a new community. Joseph understands his call only in retrospect. Forgiveness of his brothers accompanies his realization of his mission.

Hosea is called by God to mend the network of community in an even more radical fashion. He is called to marry, and what a marriage it is! On God's orders (Hos 1:2), he marries a prostitute and has three children by her. The infidelity of his wife places a heavy strain on family relationships (2:4–15). Despite everything, Hosea is to love his wife and thereby live out God's attitude to Israel (3:1). The mission of the prophet here embraces his way of life and his deepest feelings and relationships. In Hosea's life we are to see what kind of being God is: overlooking serious sin, giving his affection once again. The lives of those who are called are to bear witness to this God.

From the fact that despite the offenses of his people God maintains his relationship with them, it is only a small step to the truth that foreigners too, and even enemies, are accepted into this relationship with God. Foreign kings are seen as Yahweh's representatives. In Jeremiah 25:9 (and in 27:6 and 43:10), God gives the title "my servant" to the Babylonian king, Nebuchadnezzar, who has reduced Jerusalem and the temple to ruins. And in Isaiah 45:1 the Persian king, Cyrus, is given the honorary title of "anointed" or messiah (in the preceding verse Cyrus is even called "my shepherd"), whom God calls by name (45:3f.). God's calling and sending transcend the limits of nationalism and the ideas of friend/enemy.

But the divine plans are even bolder. God offers to Israel, that is, to all who believe in him, a permanent relationship in the form of a covenant. This makes of them all "a priestly kingdom and a holy nation" under a special protection that he will never withdraw (Ex 19:5f.). Closeness to God ("holy") and service of him ("priests") no longer define only a few chosen individuals but the entire people. All without distinction are invited and called by God. 1 Peter 2:9 extends this divine commitment to Christians. The *Shema Israel* (Dt 6:4f.) expresses the call of the entire community in another way. Behind the call to love God without reservation and with everything at one's disposal lies the ideal of the complete surrender of every individual to God.

Let us turn now to those who are the central figures in a call: God and those he calls (b). In the course of this book, it has become clear many times that in those whom God sends, different, almost opposed attitudes are combined in a strange way. These individuals never create their call or extort it from God; it comes to them, often against their will. At the same time, it requires their willing acceptance, their personal identification with the mission. This combination of a "passive" being-addressed (which, however, has profoundly "active" characteristics, inasmuch as it is an opening of the self and a listening) and the person's own committed action and speaking characterizes all who are called, from Moses with his objections to Ezekiel who is overpowered.

Many critics regard Genesis 12:1–3 as the first call in the Bible. At the age of seventy-five (v. 4) Abram follows God's order to surrender the threefold security of homeland, clan, and extended family and to abandon these for the sake of an unknown country. In starting off, the elderly Abram becomes a model of all those who at God's call break away from the known, the familiar. God's call and Abram's complete obedience combine to produce a universal blessing (v. 3). The following of God as Abram did contains a fullness of life.

The first book of Samuel reports two royal anointings by Samuel, those of Saul and David. The appointment of both comes from the choice of them by God, who calls them to this office despite an insignificant lineage (Saul; 1 Sm 9:21) and a youthful lack of experience and even despite absence (David; 16:11). The first time the choice is a poor one, and there are signs of this right from the outset: the future king of Israel is incapable of finding his father's straying donkeys (1 Sm 9:3, 20); he needs the advice and money of his servant (vv. 6, 8); and by his question to Samuel about the seer's house, he betrays his ignorance (vv. 18f.). Finally, the seer must call on him to get up in the early morning (v. 26). In light of so many discordant notes even at the time of his appointment, it is not surprising that Saul is a failure.

It is quite different with David, who grows slowly into his task through service and suffering, through forgiveness and struggle. Saul thought that he himself had to take the active role (not waiting for the sacrifice, 13:8ff.; making his own disposition of what was devoted to destruction, chapter 15, etc.), and he perished as a result. David experienced the same temptation (2 Sm 11 and 24), but he was able, for long stretches, to let God make the decisions. The two kings are examples of the fact that in their subsequent life those called must retain the initial "passive" attitude of being-appointed. Those who become the "doers" do not fulfill their vocation.

The call gives strength when the tasks are difficult or clashes occur. The clear and profound awareness of not having sought out the call accompanies the Servant of God on his way of suffering (Is 49:1: "The Lord called me" as subjective formulation of what is said in 42:6). In his Servant, as opposed to others among the people, God's call meets with an open ear (50:2, 4f.). Because God is faithful, his support of his chosen one never fails: it began long ago in the womb (44:1f.; 49:1) and lasts beyond death (53:10–12).

In his clash with Amaziah, priest at the royal sanctuary in Bethel (Am 7:10–17), Amos can appeal only to the fact that "Yahweh took me from following the sheep" (v. 15). His critical preaching is justified, not by any title, training, teacher-pupil relationship, or inherited vocation, but solely by God's action in laying hold of him. Only God's initiative turns Amos, a "layman," a herdsman, and a dresser of mulberry trees, into the first of the writing prophets and gives him the courage to announce God's word in a foreign place. (His native place, Tekoa, is in the southern kingdom, but he makes his appearance in the northern kingdom.) He does this in graphic language and with provocative images and plays on words. In him, too, a divine call is combined with personal commitment.

Is there still a little more that may be said about God, the source and origin of all calls (a)? The short book of Jonah tells of a unique case, in which a prophet runs away from his mission. This flight is a way that leads downward ("go down" occurs three times in Jon 1:3, 5); it also places others in extreme danger of their lives. Only in 4:2 do we learn the reason for the prophet's behavior. In his view, it is unreasonable to expect him to represent the overly kind and merciful God, who forgives even the bitterest enemies. Nineveh, the capital of the cruel Assyrians, who had destroyed the northern kingdom, is the very essence of evil. And yet it is this very city that Jonah is to rescue by his proclamation! Not only that, but God prefers its conversion to the "satisfaction" that he and his prophet are right (3:10). To his annoyance, Jonah must bear the shame of knowing that the disaster he had announced did not come to pass.

This wonderful story gives us a glimpse of how God is at the center of all vocations, but also of how very much this fact can become an irritation to those who are called. To be called by him means surrendering, among other things, many personal preferences, customs, and ideas of right and wrong, and it means becoming more and more like him who calls. This is probably the greatest challenge faced by those who are called. The biblical texts address this point when they assign Moses the role of God (Ex 4:16), when they say that Jeremiah has been sanctified from the womb (Jer 1:5), or when they demand of Hosea a love that forgives infidelity, like the love of God himself (Hos 3:1). God himself becomes visible in the lives of those he calls.

The powerful encounter with God that is usually described in the Bible at the beginning of a call points the way here. Even though fascinating phenomena occur at the outset (the burning bush in Ex 3, the seraphim in Is 6, the living creatures and the chariot on which God is enthroned in Ez 1, and so on), the thing that is decisive for those called is not these manifestations but God himself and his message. They are meant to move on, further and further, from the "how" to the "who." The further experience of God that is granted to them after their call guides them in this process

The name Prospect has been given to the last section of the discussion of each text. The subject in this section is the application of the story to the present day, as well as a glance at the subsequent lives of those called by God. The need for application arises from the compressed character of biblical calls. They are symbolic texts (in Greek the word *symbol* is based on the idea of "throwing together"), which contain a rich trove of experience in a condensed form and are to be interpreted in relation to it. In this kind of "explanation" or "ex-egesis," the correspondences and congruencies with the experiences of men and women called down the ages become perceptible. From this point of view, vocations are not to be regarded as isolated moments, even though many gripping biblical descriptions may give this impression. Rather, they are connected with the entire life of the one called and also with the experiences of other called persons.

A glance at the subsequent lives of those called by God has shown that a vocation essentially includes not only the glorious beginning but also perseverance in everyday life. It is there, in the carrying out of the commission, in dealings with the people, in conflicts with adversaries, that the rightness of a vocation is decided. The Old Testament does not hide the fact that it can go wrong. Some examples are Gideon, who in the end leads Israel astray into idolatry (Jgs 8:27), or Saul, who by his impatience and disobedience, his jealousy and craving for killing, throws away his election as king (1 Sm 13ff.). Other cases that belong here are the misuse of office (by Eli's sons, 1 Sm 2), the wrongful exercise of office (by Aaron's sons, Lv 10:1–7), or even the usurpation of office (by the group led by Korah, Nm 16). In all these instances the individuals were priests or Levites. Other examples of failed vocations are the so-called false prophets. These men prophecy what others want to hear (1 Kgs 22); they follow their own imagination and desires (Jer 23:16ff.; 28); they make their announcements dependent on reward (Mi 3:5ff.); and so on. A divine call at the beginning of a spiritual office is no guarantee or automatic assurance that a mission and a life will be successful.

What, then, are the criteria for showing the authenticity of a call? It is not an office or whether a person is a priest, judge, prophet, or king that makes a vocation successful. Nor is it a special role. Samson's mother, youthful Isaiah, and elderly Hannah all carry out their calls. Nor, finally, does it depend on a way of life. Hosea is called to marriage and family; Jeremiah, to celibacy (Jer 16). As a widower, Ezekiel still has a prophetic commission (Ez 24:18ff.). Amid all this variety, the decisive point is ultimately whether God holds first place in those called and can retain this absolute priority in the face of all others.

The test of this is the person's life. Those who open themselves to change and novelty without fearing for their identity can experience therein a growth of their person and their dedication. Those who are prepared for social relegation and personal brokenness win an abiding esteem and healing. Those who remain available to God in everything will, through their own blindness, lead others to light and salvation as the Servant of Yahweh does (Is 42:19, 6f.). By living in this way, those who are called are in solidarity with all those who—often even without a religious motivation—give their unreserved support to others or selflessly sacrifice themselves for them.

Calls are like crossroads, and those called are often crucified by the clashes of various groups and interests: they are at the mercy of, abandoned to, left helpless amid currents pushing in different directions. Those who persevere at the crossroads bring blessing to others. This way of life after the manner of Jesus has brought them their supreme fulfillment.

The "final movement" of the Old Testament is thus also a transition. The divine music does not stop. By way of the New Testament it continues to sound in our world and to seek hearers who will let themselves be moved to listen, sing, dance, and play their part.

11

"And, Passing By, He Saw…"
The First Disciples of Jesus

Mark 1:16–20 and 2:14–17

*T*he ministry of Jesus among his people, which lasted at most three years, is not only filled with preaching and healing but also occupied with calling and commissioning. No teacher or prophet has ever dared to bind disciples to himself and dispose of them in such a radical way as Jesus does. Not only is his claim on other human beings unique, but so too is the way along which he takes them with him. It is not a way that promises successful careers but a way that leads even to humiliation and suffering. The manner in which Jesus claims others for himself would be unintelligible if we could not see God's call at work in it.

Situation

It is as messenger of the gospel, the good and liberating news, that Jesus appears in public: "The reign of God has come near! Change your outlook and believe in the good news!" (Mk 1:15). When the reign of God is the subject of discourse, the great hopes and longing of Israel can also be heard: God will rescue his people from menacing forces, free them from suffering, and reunite them once again. The people who place themselves under his lordship and protection will experience a comprehensive peace and salvation. This reign of God has come near; indeed it is already inchoatively present in the coming and activity of Jesus.

The statement that Jesus proclaims the reign of God is a kind of descriptive title for his entire teaching and activity. The first individual event in the public activity of Jesus that Mark describes after this programmatic statement is the calling of disciples. In so doing, Mark stresses something that is characteristic of his picture of Christ: from the outset Jesus is accompanied by disciples. He never appears alone but only in the company of his followers, and he does nothing apart from them. It is already clear that he makes use of collaborators.

Structure

The two call stories in Mark 1:16–20 and 2:14 have the same tripartite structure. First, they describe the initiative taken by Jesus—his elective gaze, his turning to individuals, who are named, in their everyday situations (I); then they tell of Jesus' call to discipleship (II); and finally they show the immediate obedience to this call (III).

Mk 1:16–18	Mk 1:19–20	Mk 2:14
(I)	(I)	(I)
¹⁶And *passing by* along the Sea of Galilee, *he saw* Simon and Andrew, Simon's brother, casting (the nets) into the sea. For they were fishermen.	¹⁹And, going a little further, *he saw* James, the (son) of Zebedee, and John his brother, and (saw) them in in the boat, mending the nets.	And *passing by, he saw* Levi, the (son) of Alphaeus, sitting at the tax booth,
(II)	(II)	(II)
¹⁷And Jesus said to them: "Up *After me!* And I will make you fishers of men."	²⁰And immediately he called them.	and says to him: *Follow after me!*
(III)	(III)	(III)
¹⁸And immediately, *leaving* the nets, *they followed after him.*	And *leaving* their father Zebedee in the boat with the hired men, they went away *after him.*	And, getting up, *he followed after him.*

Interpretation

The First Pair of Brothers

In the very first verb, "pass by" (v. 16), an important theme of Mark is already discernible: the mission of Jesus, but also the life of Christians, is in the final analysis a journey. The "seeing" attributed to Jesus is not simply an awareness or an observation; it is a seeing that is attentive and interested in the person of the other. The meeting of his gaze must have been a significant experience for both parties, for otherwise it is difficult to explain why these two men spontaneously answered his call. Both of them feel a sympathy for him and experience a confidence in him that comes, as it were, at their first glimpse of him. The encounter through sight also gives them a sense that he knows and understands them in their ordinary situation. The initiative of Jesus is described in a very concise way, but it gives a sense that a relationship of trust is established. This is the basis and presupposition of the call that follows.

"Up! After me!" (v. 17) are the first words that Jesus speaks. We are not told what the basis for this demand is, but we get the impression that Jesus is himself on the way to an urgent commitment and that he will not manage it by himself. He is in immediate need of helpers to join him. The context makes it clear to the reader that the urgent need is to cry out the good news, to proclaim the message of the reign of God. Delay is no longer possible.

Jesus links a promise with the call: he will train the two brothers to become "fishers of men." Their trade as fishermen will be turned in another direction. They will be faithful to their previous work, but in a metaphorical way. Those who are called are not put under a "spell." The way of discipleship is an invitation to those called, asking them to make their previous abilities fruitful in a new way. The image of "fishers of men" may perhaps have negative associations for readers: capturing in a net suggests a deprivation of freedom. But the reference of the metaphor is positive, for it alludes (as does the parable of the net in Mt 13:47) to the biblical promise that the scattered people of God will be gathered together. Jesus will enable the two brothers to proclaim the reign of God in such a way as to give rise to a movement of gathering.

"Immediately" (v. 18; one of Mark's favorite words) they answer the call, leaving their nets behind. Their behavior is exemplary for all vocation stories. Answering the call of Jesus is tied to an abandonment. One must be able to leave something behind and gain distance from it in order to be free for the one who calls. The verb "follow after," which is important in the gospel of Mark and signifies always and only the relationship to Jesus, contains an image: one person goes ahead of the others.

The Second Pair of Brothers

By describing another call so soon afterward, Mark emphasizes the magnitude and importance of the work for which Jesus is seeking collaborators. As in the first call, the call here is to brothers. The fact that at the beginning pairs of brothers, not single individuals, are called to follow Jesus may be viewed as a symbol, a first echo of the fact that the people of God who are brought together by Jesus are stamped with the mark of brotherhood and sisterhood. Later on the disciples too will be sent out in pairs and not singly. As a result, their witness becomes more weighty (compare the joint appointment of Aaron when Moses is called, Ex 4). Jesus does not call persons to an existence as soloists or singles. He brings together those called and thus creates a community.

The initiative taken by Jesus is once again described as his elective "seeing" (v. 19). Again his gaze falls on an everyday situation. In the first story Simon and Andrew were described as they began their work (they were casting the nets). The second pair of brothers is shown at the end of their work (mending the nets). This is perhaps an accidental detail of the story, but it does indicate that a call can come in any ordinary situation. In the call to follow that is "immediately" issued, the word *call* (Greek: *kaleô*), an important one in the Bible, is now used. The abandonment no longer applies merely to things (nets) but also to persons (the father). The "leaving" has for its counterpart the opposite movement, "after him." Is this a temporary abandonment and leaving, or is it permanent? Such questions must remain open for the moment; the text says nothing about them.

Levi

The same geographical setting is already enough to show that this short narrative is akin to the two preceding stories. Jesus' "passing by" again occurs "by the sea" (v. 13). Jesus "sees" Levi at his toll booth occupied with his business, tax collecting, which was not very highly esteemed by devout Jews in comparison with the trade of fishermen. It was a business that more often than not tempted its practitioners to exploit people and collect more than was ordered by the law (compare Lk 3:13).

The gaze of Jesus is not a critical one but an elective seeing. His action again gives rise spontaneously to a relationship of trust that is the presupposition for the immediate answering of the call and the accompanying abandonment of a previous trade ("he got up"). The action of calling is described in an extremely concise way and without details. All the more crucial, then, is the decisive verb used twice: *"Follow me!"* "And he *followed* him."

The significance of this call is brought out at the meal that follows in Levi's house. "Many tax collectors and sinners" are reclining at table with Jesus and his disciples. The Pharisees take offense at this: "He eats with tax collectors and sinners" (v. 16). What Jesus is doing is incompatible with their customs and religious prescriptions.

Jesus answers: "It is not the healthy but the sick who need a physician. I have come to call not the righteous but sinners" (v. 17). His words are an interpretation of his entire preaching and mission. He has come to call and commission human beings, especially those who in the opinion of others are not to be numbered among the "righteous." Levi is an example of such persons. An encounter with Jesus and his summoning gaze is at the same time an encounter with a physician. A saving event is beginning. It has to do, at a deep level, with the damage done and the wounds incurred in the course of a person's life and with disruptions in the relationship between a human being and God. Today still, those called learn that nearness to Jesus heals their wounds. They also acquire the courage to examine their unhealthy situation.

Does Jesus need Levi, too, as a collaborator? Jesus does not take him, as he does the two pairs of brothers, into the inner circle of disciples. Levi is not even mentioned again later on. From Levi we see that there are different kinds of vocations and that the following of Jesus can also take place in a hidden way. But Levi's call does show, in an exemplary way, that a vocation is also an expression of healing and merciful love.

In Mark, Jesus is not a teacher and wonderworker who is, in addition, surrounded by a circle of supporters and disciples. Instead, from the beginning of his activity, he calls men to follow him in order that he may prepare and train them for a specific task. The call of the disciples cannot be classified as an ordinary rabbi-disciple relationship or as the relationship between a (political) leader and his crowd of supporters (a relationship based on slogans, with the supporters remaining anonymous; compare Acts 5:36–37). Instead, it is unique in its radicalness: a strict sharing of life, way, and destiny with Jesus).

At the literary level (but also at a deeper level), the calls of the disciples bring to mind 1 Kings 19:19–21, the call of Elisha by Elijah (see Chapter 5, above). Elijah finds Elisha, too, in an ordinary situation. Elisha's farewell meal can be compared with the meal in the house of Simon and Andrew (Mk 1:29–31) or the banquet given by Levi. From this comparison we learn that something just as important happens in the call of the disciples as happened in that call of a prophet. Like Elisha, the disciples receive the dignity and mission of a prophet.

Perspectives

At the appointment of the Twelve later on, in Mark 3:14–15, the goal and purpose of the calling of the entire group of disciples are made known. The group of apostles is a prophetic sign and symbol of the entire new people of God. All who follow Jesus have, fundamentally, the same destiny as the apostles. According to 3:14–15, the first and most important characteristic of disciples of Jesus is that they "are with him" and live in community with him. The second characteristic is grounded in the first: they are to continue the mission of Jesus and, like him, to proclaim the reign of God and heal human beings of their illnesses (the two are intrinsically connected).

In his chapter of parables (4) Mark shows that "to be with him" opens the way to the "mystery" of the reign of God (4:11). The latter is at the same time the mystery of Jesus himself, for with him and in his person the reign of God draws near. No one can understand Jesus and the reign of God "from outside," from a skeptical distance and by looking for external proofs (see 4:12), but only by getting involved with him in an entirely personal way. It is only in the inner space created by the following of Jesus that human beings come to know who Jesus really is. Discipleship is the way to the understanding of Christ.

When those who "are with him" are also sent out (a first instance of this is described in Mk 6:7–13), they communicate to others what they have learned about the person of Jesus and the reign of God from their fellowship with him (not propositions of faith or moral principles, but the mystery of his person).

Those who are called not only continue the mission of Jesus but also act according to his way of thinking. This is shown in "abandoning" and "serving."

Abandonment

Mark does not mention any *special* conditions for the following of Jesus (education, talents—the first disciples are simple fishermen); he mentions only readiness to abandon something "for his sake." What is meant is not only things and human relationships, but even the person's very self. The clearest expression of this is in Mark 8:34–38. This abandonment, as well as the poverty in which the disciples who have been sent out come to people (6:8–9), are not, as such, a value or an ideal, but are intelligible only in reference to the reign of God and the person of Jesus. The disciples will be recompensed "a hundredfold" for all that they now do without (10:28–30).

Service

The importance of this attitude is already clear from the fact that Jesus speaks of it twice, each time in connection with a quarrel among the disciples concerning a hierarchy among them (Mk 9:35; 10:42-45). The word *serve* (Greek: *diakonein*) originally refers to service at table. It is thus a service not of an object or an idea but of concrete persons.

Not only does Jesus instruct the disciples ("Whoever wishes to be great among you must be your servant," 10:43), but he also lives out this attitude of service to the point of surrendering his life: "The Son of Man came not to be served but to serve, and to give his life as a ransom for many" (10:45; like 2:17, this saying sums up his entire mission). The disciples of Jesus who live according to his mind are to go on being a "ransom" for a human race that is in many respects enslaved and unfree.

More than the other evangelists, Mark emphasizes the lack of understanding in those whom Jesus calls. He describes them in situations in which it is difficult for them to understand Jesus or in which their trust in him is weak, especially when he alludes to the path of suffering that lies ahead of him. When Mark speaks, sternly and without any glossing over, of the disciples' inadequate understanding and scant faith, he is saying, indirectly:

(a) It is not easy to understand Jesus and the mystery of his person. The difficulty is partly due to the way in which he makes his appearance on the scene. He does not demonstrate his divine sovereignty in such a way as to make any doubt impossible; he comes, instead, as the Son of Man, as one of us.

(b) It is, on the other hand, utterly crucial that his disciples come to know the person of Jesus. According to the gospel of Mark, discipleship is a long and laborious schooling in understanding.

A high point in the disciples' lack of understanding appears in the passion narrative. Peter denies his master (14:66–72) instead of courageously confessing him and thereby denying himself (8:34). All of the disciples, who have previously abandoned everything for his sake, now leave him in the lurch and flee (14:50). The female disciples, the women who were already following Jesus in Galilee, act differently. They are with him and stand by him until his death (15:40–41).

But the following of Jesus does not end in flight and complete failure. It begins anew after the Easter event. Mark does not report any appearance of the risen Jesus, but he does end with the promise that is given by the angel to the women at the empty tomb and is intended for the disciples who had fled: "He is going before you to Galilee; you will see him there" (16:7, in fulfillment of 14:28). This "going before" is once again matched by a "following after." As formerly in Galilee, so now the beginning of discipleship depends on the initiative of Jesus—but this time the risen Jesus.

The promise, "He is going before you," is in the present tense. Anyone who has read the gospel of Mark as far as this passage senses that the words also apply to his or her own present time. The gospel is not simply a story about past encounters with Jesus. It is also meant to affect us today in the situations of our lives. Jesus has no other hands and no other feet but ours. The open-ended conclusion of this gospel leads back to its beginning and to the call of the disciples in 1:16–20. The path of the following of Jesus today is traced in advance in the path of the earthly

Son of Man and of those persons who follow after him, beginning in Galilee. The Easter faith involves the conviction that the risen and exalted Christ is no other than the earthly Jesus. He remains true to himself. Today he still seeks human beings who will continue his joyous message and saving activity in our world.

But how can we come to know him who, even today, is "passing by" (1:16)? How can we meet his elective gaze and hear his call? There is no easy answer, but we can try, in two ways, to become hearers. If, on the one hand, we listen to and meditate on what the Bible tells us of Jesus, and if, on the other, we are sensitively aware of our own situation in life, then we may receive this gift: the biblical text will resonate in us; that is, it will find an echo in us and speak to us personally.

QUESTIONS FOR REFLECTION

Have I ever sensed the gaze of Jesus? Do I long for it? Do I let myself be seen by him?

Is my focus on my own capabilities ("I can do it," "I want to/must manage it")? Am I ready to let my polarity be reversed?

What do I learn from the fact that Jesus calls immature, fallible human beings and from his patience with their lack of understanding?

Have I been called once and for all, or does a vocation also mean being sent on my way and learning as I go?

12

"What Must I Do to Inherit Eternal Life?"
The Following of Jesus and the Problem of Riches

Mark 10:17–31

The calling of disciples in Galilee at the beginning of Jesus' public ministry evidently raises no difficulties. These calls are ideal cases. The situation is different in the following incident, which occurs at the end of the activity of Jesus shortly before his entrance into Jerusalem. Is the call of a disciple frustrated by attachment to wealth and possessions?

Situation

The story of a rich man who comes to Jesus with a question (vv. 17–22) and the ensuing conversation between Jesus and the disciples (vv. 23–31) form a unit. Just before this incident, other people turned to Jesus with questions (Mk 10:2, 10). Parallel versions of our two-part pericope are given in Matthew 19:16–30 and Luke 18:18–30. There too, as in Mark, they follow directly on the scene in which people bring children to Jesus. The evangelists thus set up a contrast between the rich man's question and the words of Jesus about the children. In the final analysis, salvation is achieved not by our own activity but by receiving it as a gift and with the attitude of children.

Only in Matthew is the questioner a young man who inquires specifically about the good that he must do in order to have life (Mt 19:16) and is convinced that he still lacks something beyond the observance of the commandments (19:20). The invitation to discipleship is his if he wants to be perfect (19:21).

In Luke the questioner is a prominent individual (Lk 18:18), who at the end must hear Jesus' stern words about the rich (v. 24). In another passage, Luke tells of the meeting of Jesus with a teacher of the law who asks him exactly the same question as the prominent individual: "Teacher, what must I do to inherit eternal life?" (10:25). In the one encounter the evangelist describes the following of Jesus as the way to life (18:22); in the other, he stresses love of neighbor as the entrance to life (10:28–37). The two are intrinsically connected.

Structure

The following outlined overview is meant to show how the two parts of our pericope (vv. 17–22 and 23–31) are interrelated both literarily and thematically.

v. 17   Jesus is on the *road,*
            a man runs up to him and falls on his knees before him.
            His question: "What must I do to inherit eternal *life?*"
vv. 18–19   Jesus answers: "No one is good but *God* alone.
            You know the commandments…"
v. 20   The man is emphatic: "I have kept all these from my youth."
v. 21   Jesus *looks at* him and loves him.
            "You lack one thing: Sell what you have…*follow me.*"
v. 22   He goes away sad (reason: his *riches*).
vv. 23–26   Jesus looks around.
            He says to the disciples: "How difficult it is for the *rich* to enter the *kingdom of God!*"
            Consternation of the disciples ("Who can be saved?")
v. 27   Jesus *looks at* them.
            "Everything is *possible for God."*
v. 28   Peter is emphatic: "We have left everything and *followed you.*"

vv. 29–31   Jesus promises a reward for discipleship, and eternal
              life.
v. 32   Jesus on the *road* to Jerusalem (third prediction of the
              passion, vv. 33–34).

The entire passage is framed by the theme of the road (vv.
17 and 32). The road from Galilee to Jerusalem is a symbol of the
way followed by the Son of Man in proclaiming the good news
and in his attitude of healing and serving. Although this way
becomes a way of suffering because Jesus meets with rejection, it
is at the same time the way into eternal life. In this context discipleship means following Jesus on his particular way.

The central concepts of our pericope—"eternal life" and
"kingdom of God"—are not simply juxtaposed but are intrinsically interrelated. Mark has already shown that the attainment of
eternal life is the same as entrance into the kingdom of God (see
9:43, 45–47).

The first part of the pericope (vv. 17–22) begins with a man
who comes running to Jesus in search of eternal life and ends with
the man shocked and sad as he leaves Jesus. In the second part,
the conversation between Jesus and the disciples (vv. 23–31),
there is a change in the opposite direction. The initial consternation of the disciples turns into a firm confession of Jesus. The
final words of the seeker to Jesus are the statement that he has
kept the commandments (v. 20); the words of the disciples are cli-
maxed by the statement of Peter, their spokesman, that they have
followed Jesus (v. 27). The final words in both instances have the
undertones of a question.

In both parts of the passage Jesus speaks of God. In the first,
he stresses the point that God alone is good; in the second, he
emphasizes the omnipotence of God. The references to Jesus' looking at the questioner (v. 20) and the disciples (v. 27) are the center
of the story in both parts. The following of Jesus, together with the
abandonment of everything, is presented in the first part as an invitation to further discussion, and in the second as a statement. Great

possessions are the reason why the seeker goes away sad. The motif of riches is also the occasion for the growing consternation of the disciples. The two-part pericope begins with a question about eternal life and ends with the promise of this life.

A first reflection on the structure of the text already brings out some central themes: deep longing for eternal life and the kingdom of God, and the following of Jesus as the way to this life. Successful discipleship does not depend on human preconditions but on the elective initiative of Jesus ("looking at") and on God's powerful action.

Interpretation

Verse 17: The disciples, who are on the road with Jesus, must get the impression that this man has some very important and urgent concern. He runs up to Jesus and falls on his knees before him—a gesture accompanying a deeply felt request (see 1:40). He asks, not with a single question but several times and intensely (the verb in the original text is in the imperfect tense): "What must I do to inherit eternal life?" He is a seeker. Only at the end and almost in passing does the reader learn that he is rich and has many possessions. He seems to be unsatisfied by his wealth and unable to find meaning and existential fulfillment in it. His desire and interior longing is for eternal life. As the address, "Good Teacher," shows, he esteems Jesus highly. He is convinced that Jesus can give him reliable information on a problem that he feels urgently. There is a song that says: "Let your deepest longing be your best adviser." Material riches and nonmaterial ones as well, such as talents and relationships, can blind. Jesus wants us to open our eyes to the "more."

Verses 18–20: Jesus redirects the respect paid him; it belongs not to him but to another. God alone is good, and he alone can, in his goodness, bestow the desired life. When Jesus points to the commandments (the Decalogue), he does so not because persons can by their observance earn or ensure this life, but because their observance is one way they can respond to God's goodness.

The man, whose name we do not learn, says, "Teacher, I have kept all these since my youth." He has, in fact, reason to be satisfied. Since his childhood he has led a religious life, and he is now in a good financial and social position. In keeping with biblical piety, he could see in this prosperity a sign of God's blessing. Why then does he turn to Jesus with his urgent question? Has the way in which Jesus preaches the gospel of God's kingdom awakened a dissatisfaction with the past and given rise to a new quest?

Verse 21: The conversation on theology turns into an encounter at the human level. The teacher not only listens attentively to the questioner, but "looking at him, he loved him." This is the only place in Mark in which Jesus' affection for a human being is expressed by the verb *love* (Greek: *agapaô*). His loving interest in the person of this seeker is the key to the invitation that follows. This invitation may be paraphrased thus: "Come with me! I need you for proclaiming the good news! You, a man who has accomplished something in his life, who is successful in his calling and leads a good religious life, but who is yet not satisfied with what he has achieved and in whom an unbridled quest of eternal life has been awakened."

Jesus says to the man, "You lack one thing," not only because he wants him as a fellow worker but also because he loves him. The one thing in which he falls short is an abiding closeness to Jesus, a being-with-him, or discipleship. But one can follow Jesus on his way only if one is ready to leave something behind. In other call stories, individuals immediately and spontaneously leave everything behind at Jesus' call in order to follow him on his way without anything to hold them back (Mk 1:16–20). Here, however, a man is explicitly challenged to abandonment: "Go, sell what you have, and give [it] to the poor, and you will have treasure in heaven, and come, follow me!"

Verse 22: The reason this man—"shocked at the words"—
goes away sad is his economic and professional ties: "For he had
many possessions."

Verses 23–26: At the beginning of the new scene eye contact
as the sign of a personal relationship is once again mentioned:
"Jesus looked around." His gaze now directed at the disciples who
surround him. He struggles with a problem and says to them,
"How hard it will be for those who have wealth to enter the kingdom of God!" A little later he emphasizes the point: "Children,
how hard it is…!" It seems even to be impossible. Jesus makes the
problem more difficult still with the image of the camel and the
needle's eye, a proverbial expression of impossibility. Repeatedly
and with increasing intensity, the disciples express their consternation. Beside themselves with fear, they say to one another, "Then
who can be saved?" Like the rich man, the disciples themselves are
profoundly shocked. Do they doubt even their own salvation?

Verse 27: "Looking at them" (the same verb as in v. 21), he
says to them, "For human beings it is impossible, but not for God;
for God everything is possible." The manner of his gaze expresses
his personal affection for them and encourages his disciples to
believe in this God. To reach God's kingdom, inherit life, and find
salvation—this is, humanly speaking, an impossibility. Human
beings cannot, by their own efforts and achievements, merit access
to salvation. Furthermore, riches are a great hindrance on the way
to salvation. That a human being should reach the kingdom of God
is a gift of God and depends on his active power. When all is said
and done, one can only receive this undeserved gift in the manner
of children (Mk 10:15). Even the following of Jesus, this special
way to life, is made possible by God. When for the sake of Jesus
one attains to a new attitude toward property and possessions, it is
not the result of one's own heroic decision, but God's doing.

Verses 28–31: When Peter says, "Look, we have left everything and followed you," Jesus answers with a promise. The abandonment of possessions and even of human ties, which the
disciples accept for the sake of Jesus and the good news, is out of

proportion to the promised reward. The disciples will experience this reward initially ("now in this age") and definitively in eternal life ("in the age to come").

Those who renounce whatever creates unnecessary ties and who learn to relativize what is superficially important are gifted in many ways and experience an entirely different and permanent form of riches: the nearness of God, profound relationships with the neighbor, joyful contentment with themselves. A new world opens up. Everything belongs to those who are loved by God.

Perspectives

The rich man who asks Jesus what he must do to obtain eternal life was in principle chosen to bear witness to that life as a disciple. Jesus would gladly have had him as a fellow worker. Does he miss out on an opportunity that will not come again? Is he an example to warn others? Is Mark here offering a call story that has a negative outcome? We would be glad to know how this man fares later on.

Readers of Mark's gospel ask themselves, somewhat shocked, whether the way to the kingdom of God and eternal life consists generally and for all in a following of Jesus that involves a radical renunciation of possessions and even of family ties. But even within the gospel of Mark we note that there are various ways of being united to Jesus and of abandoning possessions and relationships. Some women are said to follow Jesus and serve him, presumably with their private means (15:40–41). Bartimaeus, the blind beggar who after being cured follows Jesus on his way (10:52), leaves behind his one cloak. The possessed man at Gerasa, after being cured, asks Jesus permission to remain with him, although the request is not granted. Instead, Jesus instructs him to proclaim to his own circle of friends the divine mercy that he has experienced in his healing (5:18–20).

One thing is clear: the direction taken by Jesus on the way to life and to God's kingdom is for everyone. He embodies this way in his very person. All are, in addition, meant to bear witness to the gospel and to Jesus. No one is excluded from his personal affection. The following of Jesus is possible for all, even if in different, individual forms.

In one passage, the gospel of Mark makes a programmatic statement of what Jesus expects from everyone in this regard: "If any want to become my disciples, let them deny themselves and take up their cross and follow me" (8:34). All are not called to renounce possessions in the same manner, but all must practice this abandonment of self, a readiness to distance themselves from their own egos and to put their own wishes and plans last. This readiness is especially tested when the confession of Jesus provokes resistance or hostility. The following of Jesus can then become a following of the cross. But, paradoxical though it sounds, those who lose their own lives for the sake of Jesus and the good news will save them (v. 35). The phrase "for the sake of" is the same one that is used in Mark 10:29 in the promise Jesus gives to Peter and his companions. Every commitment to the good news of God's kingdom will be rewarded.

Over against this call to discipleship stands the conviction of Jesus that when human beings try, even with all their strength, to safeguard their lives and rescue them for themselves, they will ultimately lose them (8:35). This leads to the unsettling question: "For what will it profit them to gain the whole world and do harm to their life? Indeed, what can they give as a ransom for their life?" (8:36–37).

The word *ransom* echoes Psalm 49. The person praying this psalm is preoccupied with the problem of wealth. What is going on in people who trust in their riches and boast of their great wealth (v. 6)? When death comes, no one can take their possessions with them (v. 17), but all must leave their wealth to others (v. 10). No one can use earthly riches to ransom themselves or others from death and to live on after death (vv. 7–9). Instead, the person praying places his trust in God: "But God will ransom my soul from the power of Sheol (= realm of death), for he will remove me from it" (v. 15).

Perhaps the rich man who comes to Jesus is a seeker like this person praying the psalm: a man who senses that he cannot, for all his riches, earn life after death. In any case, the rich man does have a glimpse of the messianic role of Jesus as mediator of eternal life. Nothing is said to prevent our thinking that later on, even if not now, he will find the way to eternal life by a consistent following of Jesus.

QUESTIONS FOR REFLECTION

What have I, in fact, left behind in order to follow Jesus? What ought I give up?

Am I able, in childlike fashion, to expect everything from God? Does this attitude attract me or rather do I think it naive?

What motivates me more strongly when I try to involve myself with Jesus: the demands connected with discipleship, or the affirming confidence of being on the way to eternal life?

Do I grasp the unity between the following of Jesus and love of neighbor? Does the call of Jesus open me to others?

13

"Let It Be Done to Me According to Your Word"
Mary as Prototype of Faith

Luke 1:26–56

C an we number Mary, too, among those called? The annunciation of the birth of Jesus certainly entails a special election and task for Mary. But God's action with her can also be interpreted as a vocation, comparable to the way in which prophets and other savior figures were called, and it can be associated with other stories in which a miraculous birth is promised. Literary similarities are already discernible: many elements in the account of the annunciation of the birth of Jesus (Lk 1:26–38) are comparable to those in the story of Gideon's call (Jgs 6:11–24), in the story of the promise of the birth of Isaac (Gn 18:1–15), as well as in the story of the birth of Samson (Jgs 13). Not only is Mary called to a special kind of motherhood, but she also assumes a prophetic role in that her life is a model of what faith means and in that her life becomes a sign by which the poor and the lowly, in particular, can see what God's attitude toward them is.

Situation

The most important passages are the meeting of Mary and the angel (Lk 1:26–38) and Mary's meeting with Elizabeth (1:39–56). The two texts have their place in the artfully shaped construction that is Luke 1—2, in which two story lines run parallel: the one that reaches from the announcement of the birth of John to the account of his birth and childhood; the other that begins with the announcement of the birth of Jesus and runs through the description of his birth and into his childhood. The two lines meet in the account of the meeting of Mary and Elizabeth, which is at the same time a first meeting of John and Jesus, and this even before their births.

Structure

The basic structure of the two texts—the annunciation and the visitation—displays comparable elements:

Luke 1:26–38	Luke 1:29–56
26–27: Gabriel is sent to Mary in a city of Galilee (Nazareth)	39: Mary hastens to Elizabeth in a city of Judah
28–29: *Greeting*	40–44: *Greeting*
37–38: The angel's promise	45: Elizabeth's glorification of Mary
38a: *Mary's answer* (consent)	46–55: *Mary's answer* (Magnificat)
38b: The angel departs	56: Mary returns home

The greeting and the reaction of the one greeted are especially emphasized in both stories. The beatitude spoken by Elizabeth refers to the promise of the angel. Both meetings end with a response of Mary in which she describes herself as a servant of the Lord.

Interpretation

Faith Like Abraham's (Lk 1:26–38)

The very greeting of the angel (v. 28) already indicates that Mary's task and dignity are not based on any preconditions in her but on God's gift to her. She is the "favored one" and, as Elizabeth will say later, the woman "blessed" beyond others (v. 42). As in the case of many great biblical figures whom God takes into his service, the entire future is marked, on the one hand, by the promise, "The Lord is with you" (v. 28), and, on the other, by the encouragement given subsequently by the angel, "Do not be afraid" (v. 30). After Mary's reaction to the greeting (she is frightened by it and wonders about its meaning, v. 29), there follows the promise of the birth of Jesus and of his messianic mission (vv. 30–33). To Mary's question ("How can this be?") the angel gives a threefold answer: (a) God's Spirit and God's power will effect what from the human point of view is impossible (v. 35); (b) God has manifested his miraculous power to Elizabeth as well (v. 36; see v. 58: He has "made great" his mercy to her); (c) Like Abraham and Sarah of old, Mary must trust that God will carry out what he promises (v. 37).

In our context, this third part of the answer deserves special attention. The angel says, literally, "Every word will not be powerless for God" (v. 37). Mary and every reader with a good knowledge of the Bible will be reminded of the promise of Isaac's birth that was given at Mamre: "Is a word impossible [or: too wonderful] for Yahweh?" (Gn 18:14). In the Greek translation (the Septuagint) this passage reads: "Is any word perhaps powerless for God?" Not only does the angel allude to that scene in the words he uses, but he also wants to move Mary to trust, as Abraham and Sarah did, that every word coming from God will be completely carried out, even if it has to do with things that are beyond human assumptions and possibilities. It was, realistically, completely out of the question for Abraham and Sarah to have a child at their great age. If the two nonetheless accepted God's promise and counted on its being fulfilled, this was "against all hope, full of hope" (Rom 4:18). Abraham's attitude was the attitude of faith (Gn 15:6).

The meeting of the angel and Mary ends with Mary's free consent: "Behold [I am] the maidservant of the Lord; let it be done to me according to your word" (v. 38). Her description of herself as "maidservant of the Lord" corresponds to the expression "servant of God" that is used to describe such great biblical figures as Abraham, Moses, David, and especially the prophets. A servant or maidservant of God is a human being who is chosen by God for a special service, who cannot act as he or she desires but is at God's disposal, and who, at the same time, is under the protection of the Lord and knows that he or she belongs to him and is sheltered in him. Like the prophets, Mary freely puts herself at the service of the mighty word of God; even more, she allows it to be done to her. Today those who place themselves at God's disposal are still under his special protection.

God Remembers His Promise to Abraham (Lk 1:39–56)

As in the preceding story, so too in Mary's visit to Elizabeth, the greeting is especially emphasized (vv. 40–44). Once again we find a reference to the reliable word of God (v. 45). The conversation ends, once again, with an answer from Mary in which she expresses her understanding of herself as "maidservant of God." This time, however, her answer is a very extensive one (vv. 46–55).

Elizabeth's glorification, or beatitude, concerns Mary's faith: "Blessed is she who has believed that what the Lord said to her will be fulfilled!" (v. 45). This beatitude is in contrast with the words of the angel to the pious priest Zechariah, to whom he prophesies that he will be mute for a time, "because you did not believe my words, which will be fulfilled in their time" (v. 20). Faith means trusting that what God says will certainly come to pass, even though when one looks at one's own qualifications, one cannot see how this can be. Unlike Zechariah but like Abraham and Sarah, Mary accepts God's promise and does not doubt. She has no other security and support than God's reliable word. God stands by his word and has the power to carry it out. This is the experience of those who, like Mary, rely on God.

Mary's answer to Elizabeth's beatitude is the Magnificat (vv. 46–55), a hymn of praise to God that is expressed in her people's language of prayer. One verse of it is addressed to Elizabeth as well: "Surely, from now on all generations will call me

blessed" (v. 48). The basis of this future universal expansion of
the beatitude is, in Mary's eyes, the great things (Greek: *megala*)
which the Mighty One (Greek: *dynatos*) has done for her. Even
though to the outward eye not very much has happened yet, and
even though Mary has thus far only been able, strictly speaking,
to verify the truth of what the angel had said about Elizabeth, the
words of verse 48 are Mary's profession of belief that no word of
God is powerless or ineffective (Greek: *adynateô;* see v. 37). She
is already convinced that God has done great things in her life,
and this is the occasion for magnifying God (Greek: *magalynô*) in
joyous praise (v. 46).

As the Savior (v. 47) deals with her, so he has previously
dealt with others in the history of her people, beginning with
Abraham. Mary connects her experience with the history of her
people, and she has a bold prophetic vision of God's way of acting. As in the past, so in the future God will show his care for his
people. This prophetic vision is also at work when, in the second
half of the Magnificat, Mary describes God's action in the past
tense (e.g., "He has brought down the mighty from their thrones
and lifted up the lowly; he has filled the hungry with good things
and sent the rich away empty," vv. 52–53). The future is here
being described as though it had already come to pass. This manner of speech expresses the anticipation that God's promises will,
with utter certainty, be fulfilled.

Mary is herself a prophetic sign of the way in which God
continues to act. As God has looked with favor on the lowliness of
his maidservant (v. 48), so he will look after his servant, Israel (v.
54). As Mary in her lowliness has experienced God's loving attention, so God will continue to turn his face to the lowly and exalt
them (v. 52). The description of Israel as servant of God raises
echoes of the great prophetic images of hope (e.g., Is 41:8–9).
God will continue to care for his people, raise them up, and gather
them. In doing so, he will be remembering his promise to Abraham. Later on, this will be the experience especially of the people
who encounter Jesus: the woman, a "daughter of Abraham," who

has suffered a severe bodily affliction for eighteen years and whom Jesus heals (Lk 13:16); Zacchaeus, a "son of Abraham" (19:9), for whom Jesus' visit becomes an experience of the love of the God who seeks out and rescues the lost.

Mary's vocation, her personal way of faith as God's maidservant, is to be a model and sign of hope for the servant of God, that is, the entire people of God and all its lowly, hungry, and disadvantaged members. Not only by her words, but also by her life, she proclaims the God who deals with the entire people of God as he does with her.

The center of the Magnificat, the hinge for the change from God's action in her to his action in his people, is the thought that in his exercise of mercy, God remains faithful to himself (v. 50). No matter what happens in the history of his people, as well as in our own life history and in an unpitying and merciless world, God does not cease to be the Merciful One, for mercy is a reflection of his innermost being (see Ex 34:6–7). The lives of those who are called are still today a sign of God's unceasing favor to the lowly.

Perspectives

A Beatitude Lives On

Only in Luke do we find the following scene occurring in the public ministry of Jesus: "A woman in the crowd raised her voice and said to him, 'Blessed is the womb that bore you and the breasts that nursed you!' But he said, 'Blessed rather are those who *hear* the *word* of God and *keep* it'" (Lk 11:27–28). The voice of this woman resounds like an initial fulfillment of the prophecy in the Magnificat that from henceforth all generations shall call Mary blessed. The response of Jesus is, at first hearing, a displeasing one. But we must take as our starting point that it is not meant to be derogatory and that it indirectly raises Mary up as a model. By her life she shows in advance what it means to hear the word of God and keep it (on "keeping," see Lk 2:19, 51). This is one of the distinctive marks of her vocation and mission.

Two other passages emphasize the importance of hearing the word and obeying it. In the parable of the sower, the good soil is compared to those "who *hear the word* with an honest and good heart, *hold fast* to it, and bear fruit in patient endurance" (Lk 8:15). In the scene in which Jesus is informed that his mother and brothers want to see him but cannot reach him because he is surrounded by a great many people, he says: "My mother and my brothers are those who *hear the word of God* and *do* it" (8:21). Again, we ought to assume that the saying is not a disparagement of his mother but that it implicitly refers to her exemplary faith. Those who, like Mary, accept God's word, attain to a close, even familial relationship with Jesus. The term "word of God" is to be understood as meaning Jesus' entire preaching of the reign of God. The primary reality of being a Christian is to hear this word, accept it without reservation, hold fast to it, keep one's eyes on what it promises, and build upon its trustworthiness. Mary is the classic example of such a life. Still today, Christians can share in this "vocation" of Mary by making God's word the measure of their lives.

Persevering in Prayer with the Disciples of Jesus

Mary plays an important role in the beginning of Jesus' earthly life and again in the beginning of the church, in particular, at the gatherings of the apostles and first community in the "upper room" after the ascension of Jesus: "All, with one mind, were persevering in prayer with the women and Mary the mother of Jesus and his brothers" (Acts 1:14). Mary is simply present, closely united with those who are praying together as they advance into an uncertain future and await what Jesus has promised them (Acts 1:4). Unanimity and perseverance are important traits of this original community (Acts 2:42, 46). Once again, the emphasis is on something exemplary in Mary. It is also the last time she is mentioned.

Jesus also promised the disciples that the Holy Spirit would come upon them (1:8) and empower them to be his witnesses to the ends of the earth. Jesus thus said verbatim, to all the disciples, what the angel had once said to Mary: "The Holy Spirit will come upon you" (Lk 1:35).

QUESTIONS FOR REFLECTION

Am I ready to trust God more *than my own abilities, more than what is to be expected, humanly speaking? Am I able to trust God unreservedly, like Mary, like Abraham?*

Have I ever thanked God for my vocation? Do I feel that I have been blessed? Do I sometimes break out into spontaneous praise?

Can I admit to myself that, despite being called, I have difficulties of faith? How do I react to these?

14

"At Your Word"
Vocation to Service in the
Redemption of Humanity

Luke 5:1–11

T he words of Peter used in the title of this chapter and of the entire book express a basic attitude that is the issue in all the biblical call stories: the acceptance of a word of God with confidence that it will be fulfilled. Such an acceptance is the beginning of something new and unanticipated.

Situation

The call of the first disciples is described differently by Luke than by Mark and Matthew. It is also introduced at a different place in the structure of the gospel. In Mark, the call of the disciples (Mk 1:16–20) is the first event of the public ministry of Jesus to be described in detail, after the programmatic statement that Jesus comes to proclaim the reign of God (Mk 1:14–15). The evangelist means to emphasize the fact that from the outset, even before he begins to teach and heal, Jesus is accompanied by disciples.

In Luke, the call of the first disciples is preceded by activities of Jesus that are described in detail. In the literary structure, these activities are divided between two Sabbaths. On the Sabbath at Nazareth (Lk 4:16–30) he appears as proclaimer of good news; the Sabbath in Capernaum (Lk 4:31–43) is marked by the first miracles of healing that he performs. A summary of his work (v. 44) concludes the account of this first activity that is a model of what is to come. Jesus is thus not someone unknown to the crowd that now gathers or to the fishermen who are to become his first disciples.

In Mark, Jesus takes the initiative by calling the two pairs of brothers away from their everyday situation in order to follow him. In Luke, the initiative for the following of Jesus comes from Peter and his companions themselves. Only in Luke does the call of the disciples occur in connection with a miraculous catch of fish.

Structure

In the first section of the story, Luke gives a concise description of how Jesus taught the crowd. He thereby sketches the background for the detailed story of the call and also hints at the purpose for which the disciples are called. The pericope can be divided thematically as follows:

vv. 1–3   Jesus teaches on the lakeshore
vv. 4–7   A miraculous catch of fish, and the power of Jesus' word
vv. 8–10a Simon Peter glimpses the divine majesty of Jesus
vv. 10b   The promise
v. 11   The following

Interpretation

Verses 1–3: In its literary form, the description of the scene is probably influenced by Mark 3:9 and 4:1. The reference to the crowd "pressing in" on Jesus (v. 1) suggests the strength of their desire to hear the "word of God." We may assume that this word of God had for its content the message of the reign of God. From the viewpoint of narrative technique, the mention of the fact that Jesus sees two boats on the shore and sees the fishermen washing their nets (v. 2) prepares the way for the event that follows. When it is then said that Jesus gets into the boat belonging to Simon and asks him to put out a little from the shore (v. 3), the story leaves open the question of whether Peter himself is in that boat while Jesus teaches the people from it. So too in the description of the miracle that follows (vv. 4–9), it is left undecided whether or not Jesus is riding in the same boat. This opening scene is perhaps given so tersely in order that what follows may be all the more emphasized. A theme that is important for the rest of the story is sounded here, namely, the hunger of people for the word of God. This detail also helps us understand why Jesus needs fellow workers.

Verses 4–7: This section shows the active power of Jesus and the reliability of his word. The crowd now disappears completely into the background, and interest turns to the dialogue between Jesus and Simon and to the miraculous catch with its size and abundance. The dialogue consists simply of Jesus' request to launch out again and let the nets down for a catch (v. 4), along with Simon's answer: "Master, we have labored all night long and caught nothing. But at your word I will let down the nets" (v. 5). Simon's answer contains (a) an objection (as an experienced fisherman he knows that after their vain efforts during the night it is senseless to fish during the day) and (b) an expression of trust ("at your word"). Though an expert, he allows a layman to tell him something, even though all his previous experience tells him the opposite. In this respect, he is an example of the person who is open.

According to the gospel of Luke, Simon has had previous contact with Jesus and has experienced his power (see 4:38–39, the healing of his mother-in-law). The words "at your word" echo the answer of Mary to the angel of the annunciation: "Let it be done to me according to your word" (1:38). Like Mary, Simon is here a model of faith: the acceptance of a reliable word (see also 8:15, 21; 11:28).

"At your word" remains the everlasting challenge to all who are called. Having been called upon by the divine "Thou," they are able to go against their previous experiences and convictions and enter upon new ways, even when these seem in advance to be as hopeless as, for example, fishing in the daytime. They are nonetheless enabled to do so by their experience that the word of Jesus (as in this story) has power to heal the sick and win over the people. As they move into the unknown, those who are called trust themselves to him, the power of whose words they have become aware.

The miracle (vv. 6–7) is described in detail (a great many fish; the nets begin to tear; helpers are needed; two boats are filled; the boats are in danger of sinking) and thus makes concrete the power inherent in the word of Jesus.

Verses 8–10a: Simon's reaction—falling down at the feet of Jesus, consternation because of his own unworthiness and sinfulness, and "fear" (see also Lk 4:36)—takes a form similar to that of Old Testament persons to whom an encounter with God is granted (see Is 6:5). In the miraculous catch of fish, Simon and his companions have experienced the nearness of the living God in the speech and action of Jesus. All, including those called, are invited to experience this nearness despite their sins.

Verse 10b: "Do not be afraid! From now on you will be catching people alive." The first point to be noted about this saying is that it is not a command ("You are to") but a promise ("You will be"). The expression "catching people alive" is a bit different from the expression "fishers of people" in Mark 1:17 and has a positive connotation. The verb translated "to catch alive" (Greek: *zogreô*) also has the meaning of "to leave alive." The idea of rescuing from certain destruction, of saving a life and (re)animating it, is also present. To use a modern comparison, Peter is like a man who steers a lifeboat or rescue vehicle to take part in an emergency action. Just as a person must put everything else second as long as he is involved in rescuing a life, so Peter will put everything else aside—his trade, his family, his human ties, even his very life—in the service of the good news of Jesus, which is urgent and is to be brought to the needy as a result of God's saving and healing love. The next and concluding verse speaks of this surrender.

Today, too, those who are called are sent on a rescue mission. Their tasks are not superfluous or artificial and frivolous. On the contrary, the service they render is necessary and does not permit delay or indifference or caution in the interest of one's own comfort. Those called are helping a human race that is profoundly endangered, and they travel ways that lead out of that threat to true life.

Verse 11: Jesus' teaching, his deed of power, and his promise motivate Simon and his companions to leave everything and follow him. Here, for the first time, we meet the verb *follow* (Greek: *akoloutheô*) that expresses the characteristic of discipleship and will be used often later on. The proper meaning of the verb is "to walk behind someone." As the gospel of Luke develops, it becomes increasingly clear that the disciples walk behind him who came "to seek and to save the lost" (19:10) and that they are meant to carry on this mission of Jesus.

Perspectives

To a greater extent than Mark, Luke emphasizes the necessity of leaving and letting go. One can be a disciple of Jesus only when one is determined to renounce personal possessions (14:33), to make human ties secondary (14:26), and to deny oneself to the point of willingness to suffer (9:23). The intention is not to devalue possessions, human ties, or a person's life; the point is rather that the message of Jesus is so urgent that it justifies the abandonment of everything else.

Luke stresses, more strongly than Mark, the fact that Peter's Lord will not leave him in the lurch, despite the weakness of his faith and despite his failure as a follower of Jesus (most clearly seen in his triple denial of Jesus). How dear the disciple is to the Lord is also made clear by the fact that Jesus prays for him (22:32). At the Last Supper Peter receives from Jesus a special commission: "And you, when you have once turned back, strengthen your brothers" (22:32). Part of his service in the saving of lives, a task promised to him at his calling, is the encouragement and strengthening of others and the protection of their constantly threatened faith in Christ.

The call of the disciples in Luke 5:1–11 is placed in an Easter setting in John 21:1–19. Several elements in the Lukan call story occur again in John: some individuals are in a situation of failure (these fishermen have labored in vain, catching nothing for an entire night in their boat on the sea, vv. 2–5); they rely on a few words from the risen Jesus ("cast the net to the right side of the boat, and you will find some," v. 6); the result is a marvelous, over-flowing catch of fish (v. 6). Differently than in Luke, the miracle in John is followed by a meal with the risen Jesus (vv. 7–13). As in Luke, there is again a question of a future task of Peter (to continue the role of Jesus as shepherd) and of the following of Jesus ("Follow me!" v. 19). In Luke 5:1–11 it is the earthly Jesus who is to be followed; in John 21:1–19, it is the risen Jesus. According to the gospel of John, the following of Jesus by the disciples begins, properly speaking, only after Easter (see Jn 13:36, "You will follow afterward"). Does the gospel of John deliberately transfer the tradition given in Luke 5:1–11 to the post-Easter period?

Since the New Testament recounts the same kind of calling of disciples once by the earthly Jesus and again by the risen Jesus, it confirms our assumption that this calling is something typical and that even after Easter, Jesus continues to call men and women. We are thus justified in relating some elements of the story to our present time. Jesus takes persons away from their ordinary occupations and even from situations of failure. His word has power to change the situation and to bestow in rich mea-sure what such persons did not attain by their own efforts. Today it is still granted to those who obey the word of Jesus to glimpse the divine mystery of his person. Not everyone, perhaps, is affected to the degree that Peter was; but the knowledge of Jesus, the risen Lord, and the experience of the power of his word will leave no one interiorly indifferent. Once men and women have been moved by Jesus and touched by his message, they will, like Peter, likewise be ready to leave everything in order to follow him—ready too to be drafted willingly for an urgent service, that of proclaiming to the poor the liberating good news and to the suffering the healing love of God.

QUESTIONS FOR REFLECTION

Do I hear, in the many voices around me, the voice of the risen Jesus, addressed to me?

How do I think of the way I travel in the following of Jesus? As a service of life and the promotion of life? Or only as one of giving help in urgent cases or emergencies?

Am I able to admit failure?

15

"Come and See!"
By Their Witness Believers Lead Others to Christ

John 1:35–51

*T*he gospel of John shows more clearly than the other gospels what happened after Easter. Calls from Jesus continued because his followers became witnesses to him.

Situation

The hymnlike beginning of the gospel of John (1:1–18) is followed by a second beginning in narrative form (1:19—2:11). The latter section is a compositional unit and may be structured according to a pattern of days. It includes events that cover seven days and may therefore be described as the great "first week" of the public ministry of Jesus.

On the first day (1:19–28), John the Baptist bears witness to his own person and purpose as well as to the "one who is coming" and is already present, though hidden (v. 26: "Among you stands one whom you do not know"). On the second day (1:29–34), Jesus comes to John the Baptist. This is at the same time Jesus' first appearance in public. The main content of this day is the Baptist's testimony about who Jesus really is. The result of this activity of witnessing is that on the third day (1:35–42), two disciples of John set out to get to know Jesus personally. One of them, Andrew, then brings his brother Simon to Jesus. The fourth day (1:43–51), starts with the call of Philip, who in turn gives Nathanael reasons for coming to Jesus. "On the third day" (2:1) after this—that is, at the end of this "first week"—the marriage at Cana takes place, and there Jesus works his first "sign" (2:1–11).

Just as the first two days are united by the idea of witness to Jesus, the next two days likewise have a common theme: the following of Jesus by disciples. The purpose of John's activity as witness is that persons should not only come to faith (see 1:7), but should also enter into a community with Jesus and become his disciples. Although the example of Philip shows that the gospel of John is familiar with the idea of individuals being called directly by Jesus (as in the Synoptic call stories), this gospel lays special emphasis on persons becoming witnesses for Jesus to one another and leading one another to him. As the wedding at Cana shows, those who follow Jesus are meant, first of all, to know Jesus and his "glory" (2:11).

Structure

The third and fourth days, on which individuals become mediators of a vocation for others, have a similar literary structure and include the following common structural elements: witness to Jesus is linked to a demand to see (I); those who hear the testimony make their way to Jesus (II); at the meeting the initiative of Jesus and his interest in those who come to him play an important role (III); he gives them an invitation or a promise (IV); the meeting leads to a confession (V). The following outline will illustrate this structure:

1:35–42 (Third day)

1:43–51 (Fourth day)
(V) Philip makes a confession of faith to Nathanael: "We have *found* him about whom Moses in the law and also the prophets wrote." (v. 44)

(I) John the Baptist points out Jesus: "*See,* the Lamb of God!" (v. 36)

(I) Nathanael is skeptical, and Philip invites him: "Come and *see!*" (vv. 45–46)

(II) Two of John's disciples follow Jesus. (v. 37)	(II) Nathanael comes to Jesus. (v. 47)
(III) Jesus *sees* them following him and asks them: "What are you looking for?" (v. 38)	(III) Jesus *sees* Nathanael coming to him, and says: "See, a genuine Israelite." (v. 47)
(IV) Invitation to the two who want to know where he is staying: "Come, and you *will see!*" (v. 39)	
(V) Andrew confesses Jesus to his brother Simon: "We have *found* the Anointed One." (v. 47)	(V) Nathanael confesses Jesus: "Rabbi, you are the Son of God, you are the king of Israel." (v. 49)
	(IV) Promise to Nathanel: "Greater things than these shall you see.... You *will see* heaven opened." (vv. 50–51)

Many vocations have a comparable prehistory. As a result of the testimony of others, persons come to Jesus, who then speaks to them and invites them.

Interpretation

Andrew and the Unnamed Disciple of John

As on the previous day, it is John who calls attention to Jesus as the latter is "walking by"; and again, as on the previous day, he calls Jesus the "Lamb of God" (v. 36). How well John must have spoken of Jesus, if two of his disciples are led to abandon their master and follow this unknown person! The two men probably trail after Jesus for a while.

The meeting is due to Jesus' initiative: "When Jesus turned and saw them following him, he said to them, 'What are you looking for?'" (v. 38). The verb *turn* does not signify a simple turning back but already includes a turning to them in a personal way. So too, his seeing is not simply a perceiving of them but already expresses a human contact. The focus of the sentence is on the question "What are you looking for?" At the same time, the question contains the very first (and therefore especially meaningful) words spoken by Jesus in the fourth gospel. He begins the conversation, not with a statement about himself or his message, but by letting the two men speak first. He is interested in their concerns and fosters their search. But what are they really looking for?

"Rabbi...where are you staying?" (v. 38). Their counterquestion sounds like an expression of embarrassment. Perhaps they are as yet unable to say for sure what they really expect of him. One thing, however, they are clear on: they want to get to know him. They are not interested in mere information (for example, on a theological problem) but in the man himself. If they can see where he is staying, and the manner and conditions in which he is living, this is already a first step in getting to know his person. That they already have a high opinion of him can be seen in the Jewish address, Rabbi ("my master"—the explanatory translation added in the text uses the Greek word for "teacher"). Jesus' answer, his second and last (and therefore once again important) word that day is the invitation, "Come, and you will see!" (v. 39). There is often uncertainty and embarrassment in the first steps of a vocation. It is helpful, then, to meet people whom one can trust. How they live bears witness to what moves them.

The text is extremely concise in saying that the two men come to his dwelling and that they remain there. All the more striking, therefore, is the narrative detail giving the time: "It was the tenth hour" (v. 39). We may interpret this as a way of emphasizing, in retrospect, a decisive moment in their lives: "That day, about four o'clock in the afternoon, it all began; from that point on, we were with him." Nothing further is said about the meeting. But the reader immediately learns the result of it, namely, their joyous certainty: "We have found...!" (v. 41). The seeking ends in a finding. Those who are called know their own "hour." It is the moment at which Jesus' eyes met theirs.

Our passage contains two words that look beyond the

moment and are important for vocation and discipleship generally: *follow (after)* and *remain.* When the verb *follow* (Greek:
akoloutheô) in used in verse 37 to describe how the two men went
after Jesus, it is already the technical term for the following
proper to disciples (see 1:43; 8:12). In the course of the gospel of
John, it will be seen that this kind of following is the same in
meaning as faith in Jesus (compare 8:12 with 12:46) and with
entrance into a communion of life and destiny with him (see
12:26; 13:36; 21:19).

In Greek, the verb *remain (menô)* also means "dwell." It is
used in this passage with both meanings, referring, that is, both to
the place where Jesus is staying and to the two men remaining with
him. Verse 39 is a kind of play on words: "They saw where he was
staying *(menô)* and they remained *(menô)* with him that day." Further on in the gospel of John (e.g., 6:56; 15:4–10), this verb acquires
great theological weight. Something of this can already be sensed
here. To "remain" does not mean simply an attachment to Jesus that
is meant to be lasting (this can become a standing by him in his passion); it also means an at-homeness that is his gift and is indestruc-
tible. *Remain* connotes the idea of everlastingness. Intimacy with
God makes it possible, as the years pass, for those who are called to
experience increasingly an at-homeness that is profound.

Meeting Jesus and being with him are not only a private
matter, but they motivate a passing on of the experience to others.
Andrew, one of the two men here, is as it were, compelled immediately to tell his brother Simon of what has happened to him:
"We have found the Messiah" (v. 41). In the person whom John
the Baptist has described as "Lamb of God," Andrew recognizes
the Messiah (Anointed One, Christ) for whom Israel yearns as a
mighty liberator. "Lamb" is a symbol of helplessness and nonvio-
lence. It also reminds the reader of the prophecy of the suffering
Servant of God, who is compared with a lamb that submits,
silently and defenselessly, to the violence done to it by others (Is
53:7). This image had no place in messianic expectations as
understood at this time. If Andrew is able to see the Lamb as at the

same time the Messiah, the one who comes in helplessness, as also the liberator, there can be only one explanation: his experience in his personal encounter with Jesus.

Andrew does not simply tell his brother about Jesus. He also leads this brother to Jesus (v. 42). For the latter, too, the encounter with Jesus becomes a decisive turning point in life.

Philip and Nathanael

On the fourth day, Jesus decides to set out for Galilee (v. 43). Three days later the wedding in Cana of Galilee takes place (2:1). If we connect these two pieces of information, we get the impression that the very tersely described meeting of Philip and Jesus and the words "Follow me!" (v. 43) are an invitation to come along to the wedding. This has a symbolic meaning: the following of Jesus is the way to a feast.

In literary terms, most of this day is taken up by the call given to Nathanael through Philip. As with Andrew the day before, so with Philip the encounter with Jesus leads to a confession of faith that he has "found" the one for whom all have so deep a longing. As Philip sees Jesus, Jesus is the one of whom Moses and the prophets wrote or, in other words, the one to whom all the scriptures point (v. 45). But Nathanael, to whom Philip makes this profession, has difficulties with the fact that Jesus is a son of Joseph and comes from Nazareth: "Can anything good come out of Nazareth?" (v. 46).

Nathanael's question not only makes the reader mindful of the tension, characteristic of the gospel of John, between Jesus' unique origin in God and his entirely normal origin from the people, but it also strengthens the reader in the conviction that discipleship is compatible with critical thought. Philip is unable to dispel Nathanael's misgivings, but he can move him to go to Jesus: "Come and see!" It is only this "seeing" in the form of a personal encounter with Jesus that leads to the overcoming of skepticism.

The description of this meeting begins, as on the day before, with the mention of Jesus "seeing" the person coming to him, and indeed (we may assume) looking at this person attentively and with interest. While the two disciples called on the day before wished to get to know Jesus ("Where are you staying?"), Nathanael learns that Jesus knows him ("Where did you get to know me?" v. 48). Jesus had seen him while he was "under the fig tree." The reader is not told of the circumstance to which Jesus is referring: Was Nathanael deep in study there, or in prayer? In any case, it was a significant moment for him. Overwhelmed by Jesus' knowledge of his heart, Nathanael confesses, "Rabbi, you are the Son of God! You are the King of Israel!" (v. 49). Nathanael's confession of Jesus as "King of Israel" fits in with the statement of Jesus at the beginning of their meeting: "Here is a true Israelite!" (v. 47). Nathanael proves himself to be a true Israelite because, on the one hand, he keeps an eye—though a critical one—on the messianic expectations of Israel and, on the other, he is open to Jesus.

The day before, Simon had learned that Jesus knew him, not only by name but in a deeper sense as well (v. 42). Jesus' knowledge of hearts is a characteristic trait in the picture of Christ given in the fourth gospel (see 2:23–25; 4:16–18, 29). He knows the hearts of human beings in a way that is elsewhere reserved for God (e.g., Ps 139:1–6; Acts 15:8).

As on the preceding day, the conversation ends with a promise from Jesus, and once again this has to do with a "seeing." Nathanael will experience things even greater than Jesus' knowledge of hearts: "You will see heaven opened and the angels of God ascending and descending upon the Son of Man" (v. 51). Nathanael has applied the titles "Son of God" and "King of Israel" to Jesus. Jesus now describes himself as "Son of Man" (this is his first description of himself). This mysterious expression emphasizes the fact that Jesus is fully and completely a human being, one of us. At the same time, he has a unique connection with God, as indicated by the image of heaven opening and the angels, who serve as intermediaries, ascending and descending upon him. The image may be taken as an allusion to the story of Jacob's dream (Gn 28:11–19, especially v. 12). What Jacob experienced in a dream at a particular geographical location (Gn 28:19: Beth-El = house of God), the disciples will experience through being with Jesus: the presence of God on earth.

The depth of meaning in the promise to Nathanael can be measured only against the background of what is said in the Prologue of this gospel: no human being has ever seen God (1:18). We cannot, by ourselves, know with final assurance who God really is; this knowledge becomes available to us only through Jesus. From now on, the Son of Man staying among us is the "place" in which the interior of heaven, the realm of God, becomes visible and accessible and in which human beings can experience the nearness of God and his care for the world.

The promise to Nathanael refers to the entire earthly ministry of Jesus. For the disciples, Jesus will always be the place over which heaven is open and from which divine light enters the world, as when, in a dark room, daylight penetrates through a chink. This entrance of divine light can be compared with the confession of believers in the Prologue of John: "We have seen his glory" (1:14). To see the glory of the incarnate Word means also to see heaven opened over the Son of Man. The first great "sign" that Jesus does immediately afterward at the wedding in Cana (see 2:11) becomes a symbol for the disciples of this "glory" and of the "opened heaven."

Those who gain sight of the Son of Man and his divine mystery also become capable of bearing witness to him. After the model of John the Baptist, all who are called to the following of Jesus are meant "to testify to the light" (1:7–8).

Perspectives

The events of that third and fourth day, when men who encounter Jesus become witnesses to him and lead others to him, serve as exemplars. The very same thing happens later on to the woman at the well of Jacob. In Jesus she meets a man who knows her and is aware of her personal situation and of her thirst for genuine life. The knowledge of her heart that Jesus shows moves this woman, as it had Nathanael, to a spontaneous confession of belief (4:19). Afterward, she becomes straightaway a witness to Jesus for the people of her town: "Come and see a man who told me everything I have ever done! Is he perhaps the Anointed One?" (4:29). As with John the Baptist, Andrew, and Philip, her personal witness reaches completion in her motivating others to come to Jesus, so that these others can say at the end: "It is no longer because of what you [the woman] said that we believe, for we have heard for ourselves, and we know that this is truly the Savior of the world" (4:42).

Mary of Magdala likewise becomes a witness to Christ, and this after she has encountered the risen Lord. His first words are "Woman, why are you weeping? What are you looking for?" (20:15). The reader of John's gospel is spontaneously reminded here of the very first words of Jesus: "Whom are you looking for?" (1:38). The way in which the risen Lord concerns himself with Mary and her plight and finally addresses her by name, "Mary!" (20:16), not only gives the certainty that he is alive, a certainty that transforms all her grief, but it also causes her to run off immediately to the other disciples and tell them, "I have seen the Lord" (20:18). Later on the overwhelming encounter with the risen Jesus turns the other disciples too into witnesses of the Easter message.

As we see repeatedly throughout the gospel of John, the following of Jesus begins in the experience of men and women that Jesus is concerned for them, for their questions and their suffering. At the same time, they discover in him the one to whom all the hopes in the Bible and their own personal seeking and longing refer. At the center of the gospel there stands not a particular teaching, not some kind of religious or social program, but a person. This person does not force himself on anyone, certainly not by the means power has at its service. It is as true today as it was at that time: "Among you stands one whom you do not know" (1:26). Witnesses are needed who will point him out. Just as John the Baptist turned the attention of those first two disciples to Jesus, just as later Andrew told his brother about Jesus, or as Mary of Magdala bore witness to the other disciples about her meeting with the risen Lord, so today people still come to faith in Christ because men and women who are deeply moved by him tell their story to others and bear witness to him.

As in the Synoptic Gospels, so in the gospel of John, the following of Jesus is connected with a missionary commission. This commission is understood as being, in particular, the giving of witness. But what are the signs of the right kind of witnessing?

(a) Witnesses of the right kind speak of what they have personally experienced. The content of their testimony is not one or another teaching of the faith, nor is it a religious program; rather, they speak of one whom they know from personal experience. According to John, the disciples, men and women, are called first of all to get to know Jesus. They succeed in "seeing" Jesus only if they commit themselves to the way of the following of Jesus.

(b) Witnesses of the right kind are ready to stand up for Jesus and defend him, even if this means personal disadvantage and leads to their experiencing the "hatred of the world" (15:18–19).

(c) Witnesses of the right kind identify themselves with the concerns of Jesus and make his message their own. The prime example of this is John the Baptist, who identifies himself so completely with Jesus the Light that he reflects this light and becomes so like Jesus as to be mistaken for him (1:7–8).

(d) Witnesses of the right kind do not talk about themselves or make themselves the center of attention. Their whole effort is that he to whom they bear witness may receive the attention due to him. They are ready to withdraw into the background behind Jesus, as did John the Baptist, whose mission of witnessing culminated in the words "He must increase, but I must decrease" (3:30).

(e) The goal of the testimony given by the disciples of Jesus is not only that others should come to know the one who dwells unknown in their midst (1:26), but also that they should come to him and enter into community with him.

QUESTIONS FOR REFLECTION

Do I make others aware of Jesus, and am I also ready to lead them to him? Do I allow myself to be led?

Do I believe that Jesus is really interested in me as I am and not simply in something belonging to me, for example, my capacity for work?

What image do I connect with the path of following? Primarily its difficulty? Or also its festiveness?

Do I possess both a critical mind and openness?

Do I like being a witness to Jesus?

16

Conversion or Vocation?
Paul on the Road to Damascus

Acts 9:1–30

*P*eople commonly say that Saul became Paul and speak of his being converted on the road to Damascus. But what he experienced there as a stroke of lightning out of the blue can also be classified among the biblical call stories. On the way to Damascus Paul encountered the risen Lord, and he became convinced that all believers can experience the reality of the risen Jesus, even if not in so overwhelming a fashion.

Situation

Paul describes himself as one called to be an apostle (Rom 1:1; 1 Cor 1:1). His tireless commitment to the gospel and his capacity for perseverance are understandable if we see a call story as part of his life. This story begins with the occurrence at Damascus, which overtakes him unexpectedly. To interpret correctly this decisive event, we must know a little about Paul's previous history, which was marked by religious fervor and even fanaticism. The first we hear of him is in the account of the stoning of Stephen. He is indeed only an onlooker there, but it is specifically said that he approved of the killing of that exemplary witness to Jesus (Acts 8:1). Later on, he himself proceeds with violence against those who follow Jesus and think of themselves as adherents of "the Way." He "breathes threats and murder" against the disciples of Jesus (Acts 9:1–2) and persecutes them even to death (Acts 22:4).

Why was he bent on destroying the Christian community in Jerusalem (Acts 8:3)? Why, finally, does he journey even as far as Damascus in order to imprison the adherents of Jesus who are living there? He is motivated by utter religious conviction and by zeal for his Jewish faith in God and for the Torah. He is a Pharisee, a follower of the strictest school of religious thought in Judaism. To him Jesus, who was executed as a blasphemer, is a stumbling block (1 Cor 1:23), and he finds it intolerable that anyone should regard a crucified man as the Messiah and should become his follower.

In any case, what takes place on the road to Damascus is not the conversion of a sinner who is far from God, but the call of a Pharisee who is faithful to the Law and utterly committed to his religion. Jesus, the risen Lord, meets him there. Not only does this encounter lead to a revision of his previous idea of Jesus, but during it he also receives a divine call and is accepted for special service.

The great importance of the Damascus event for Paul, and beyond him for early Christianity, can already be seen in the fact that the Acts of the Apostles recounts it three times: once at the beginning of Paul's missionary activity (Acts 9:1–30) and twice after his imprisonment in Jerusalem (22:1–21; 26:1–23). The three accounts have elements in common, but they also show specific differences and emphases.

Structure

The first account of the Damascus event and its consequences (Acts 9:1–30) can be entitled "A Persecutor of Jesus Becomes His Disciple and Witness." The main sections of the story are these:

vv. 1–2   Saul persecutes the adherents of the Way.
vv. 3–9   Encounter with Christ on the road to Damascus
vv. 10–19a Vision of Christ by Ananias, a disciple of Jesus in

Damascus. He is told to lay hands on Saul. Saul is baptized.

vv. 19b–25   Saul with the disciples in Damascus. He begins to preach Jesus in the synagogues, but after a time he is forced to flee Damascus.

vv. 26–30   Saul seeks contact with the disciples in Jerusalem. Barnabas takes his part. After debates with the Hellenists, Saul flees to Tarsus.

Interpretation

We shall look more closely not at the entire passage, but only at the actual encounter with Christ and the meetings with Ananias and Barnabas.

The Encounter with Christ (Acts 9:3–6)

A brief description of the external circumstances (v. 3) is followed by a dialogue (vv. 4–6) that forms the center of the entire passage (9:1–30). The text reads as follows:

> ³But as he was traveling, it happened that [Saul] was approaching Damascus, and a light from heaven suddenly flashed around him,
> ⁴and, falling to the ground, he heard a voice saying to him:
>   "Saul, Saul, why do you persecute me?"
> ⁵He said:
>   "Who are you, Lord?"
> But [the Lord] said:
>   "I am Jesus, whom you are persecuting.
>   ⁶But get up and go into the city,
>   and you will be told what you are to do."

"Saul" translates the Greek form of Saul's Jewish name. From Acts 13:9 on, it will always be replaced by the Latin name *Paulus,* that is, Paul. The repetition of the name, "Saul, Saul," brings out the importance of what is to be said (compare Ex 3:4). The same holds for the address "Martha, Martha" (Lk 10:41) or "Simon, Simon" (Lk 23:31) during the ministry of the earthly Jesus. "Why are you persecuting me?" Those who persecute the disciples are, in the final analysis, persecuting Jesus himself. Jesus identifies himself with his suffering disciples. The thought of this identification will become very important for the suffering Christians of all future generations. Jesus identifies himself with them too, as they are attacked and persecuted for his sake. The beatitude and promise in Matthew 5:11–12 are meant for them too.

In his answer to the (only) words spoken by Saul ("Who are you, Lord?"), the one who is appearing to him first makes himself known. He calls himself "Jesus" (without any addition such as "Christ" or "Lord"). Saul is meant to realize the identity of the Lord present to him with the earthly Jesus. Another echo of the earthly Jesus is the Aramaic address "Saul"; Jesus speaks in his mother tongue (see 26:14). The answer Jesus gives also contains a commission: Saul is to hold himself ready, in Damascus, for information on what he is to do.

Meetings with Ananias (Acts 9:10–19a)
and Barnabas (Acts 9:27)

The appearance of Christ is followed by a meeting with Ananias, a Christian of Damascus. It can even be said that the meeting with Christ is continued in a meeting with another human being. A meeting with believers is often a continuation of a divine call and helps to clarify, interpret, and take hold of this call. After three days Ananias heals Saul of the blindness caused by the Damascus event and baptizes him. From Ananias, Saul also learns in what his mission consists: Saul is a "chosen vessel," whom Christ will use to bring the "name" of Jesus to the pagan nations and to Israel (v. 15). His entire future mission is summed up in the image of a vessel containing something very precious that is to be brought to others. Those called are "filled" by God. They have the ability to pass on to others what has been given to them. In this way they bring God to human beings.

The "name" signifies the person himself, his nature and his way of thinking. It is an important theological theme of the Acts of the Apostles that redemption is given to us through the name of Jesus and through the invocation of this name (e.g., 2:21; 4:10, 12). Paul cannot evade his commission but is subject to a mysterious "must." This necessity also applies to the way of suffering that Paul must travel: he must suffer for the name of Jesus (v. 16).

Here in Damascus and later in Jerusalem, Paul publicly professes his allegiance to the one whom previously he had persecuted. Thus he is already one of the group who say of themselves, "We cannot keep from speaking about what we have seen and heard" (4:20). Basically he, like the first apostles and eyewitnesses of Jesus, has been granted an Easter experience. Outside of Damascus he had "seen the Lord" (v. 27; see 1 Cor 9:1), the risen Jesus.

In Jerusalem Paul meets Barnabas (9:27), a respected personage of the Jerusalem community. This meeting too can be interpreted as a consequence of the encounter with Christ. Barnabas's main concern is that Paul should be accepted into the circle of disciples. Those who initially are afraid of him accept him as a companion on their Way.

Perspectives

The second account of the Damascus event is part of Paul's lengthy speech of self-defense before the Jewish people on the square in front of the temple in Jerusalem (Acts 22:1–21). During his arrest he seeks to win his people to Christ. The third account is part of the speech of self-defense that Paul delivers in the presence of Festus, the Roman governor, and King Agrippa II during his imprisonment in Caesarea (Acts 26:1–23). Paul's aim in this speech is to lead pagans to belief in the resurrection.

The three presentations are not identical and show some

important differences. It is therefore all the more striking that they all contain these words from the conversation on the road to Damascus: "Saul, Saul, why do you persecute me?" "Who are you, Lord?" and "I am Jesus, whom you are persecuting." These words, then, have a special importance for the author of Acts. They signify that Paul's vocation is essentially due to the initiative of Jesus and that Jesus makes known who he really is. This knowledge corrects Paul's earlier false estimation of Jesus.

The three presentations also have in common the thought that Paul is ordered to carry out a mission. This mission is described in greater detail in the third account: Paul is appointed to be a servant and a witness to what he has seen and to what the Lord will show him in the future (Acts 26:16). Paul's entire ministry consists in bearing witness to his own experience, which includes not only his encounter with Christ on the road to Damascus but also his further encounters with Christ (see Acts 18:9–11; 22:17–21; 23:11). It is not by his own strength and efforts that Paul is able with complete single-mindedness to be a servant and witness of Christ; it is only because of the certainty that he is not alone and that Jesus himself is close to him and at his side: "Do not be afraid, but speak and do not be silent, for I am with you" (Acts 18:9–10). This promise of the Lord gives us insight into the source of Paul's strength and courage on the exceptional "way" of his following of Christ.

Luke's accounts in the Acts of the Apostles are supplemented by Paul's own testimony in his letters. In them he comes to speak, not indeed explicitly, yet clearly enough, about the Damascus event. That he speaks of it there in different ways shows that its wealth of meaning is fundamentally inexhaustible.

In 1 Corinthians Paul numbers himself among the Easter witnesses. His experience at Damascus had been of an appearance of the risen Lord: "Have I not seen Jesus our Lord?" (1 Cor 9:1; see Acts 9:27). And when giving an early Christian list of Easter witnesses, he says: "Last of all, as to one untimely born, he appeared also to me" (1 Cor 15:8; see Acts 9:17; 26:16).

According to Galatians 1:13–17 the Damascus event amounts to a divine revelation, and the call given to Paul is interpreted as a prophetic vocation: "But when God, who had set me apart before I was born and called me through his grace, was pleased to reveal his Son to me, so that I might proclaim the good news among the Gentiles…" (vv. 15–16; compare the call of Jeremiah in Jer 1:5 and of the Servant of God in Is 49:1).

In Philippians 3:4–14 the turning point in the life of Paul the Pharisee is seen as having been laid hold of by Christ and as the gift of knowledge of Christ: "More than that, I regard everything as loss because of the surpassing value of knowing Christ Jesus my Lord" (v. 8). And he adds: "I press on to make it [the knowledge of Christ and communion with him] my own, because Christ Jesus has made me his own" (v. 12).

In these three passages Paul speaks in different ways of an Easter experience, a revelation, and a knowledge of Christ. That he is alluding to his encounter with Christ on the road to Damascus is already clear from the fact that in the context of each passage he calls to mind his earlier persecution of Christians. He had persecuted the community (1 Cor 15:9; Gal 1:13; Phil 3:6), and he did so as a "zealot" (Gal 1:14; Phil 3:6).

Anyone reading the Acts of the Apostles and the letters of Paul gets the impression that the overwhelming event at Damascus has to do with Paul's, but not with the reader's, own life. And yet Paul makes it clear, especially in the letter to the Philippians, that his vocation is not an isolated occurrence but contains elements, exemplary traits, that play a role in the vocation of every Christian.

In the letter to the Philippians Paul speaks of "the surpassing value of knowing Christ Jesus my Lord" (3:8). This can be confirmed by all Christians who have been given an inkling of who their Lord is and how precious he is to them, and who have in any way been "made his own" (see 3:12). "Knowledge" is not something solely of the intellectual realm alone; it is based, at the deepest level, on a personal closeness that echoes in the desire to "gain" Christ and to "be found in him" (3:8–9). To know Christ means also to experience "the power of his resurrection." The experience is accessible only to those who know a "sharing in his sufferings" (3:10).

Paul looks upon his own way as a running toward a goal, "the victory prize of the call of God that leads upward in Christ Jesus" (Phil 3:14). He asks others to follow the same way: "Join in imitating me!" (3:17).

The second letter to the Corinthians likewise has a passage suggesting that what Paul experienced in his vocation every Christian can also experience in his or her own life, perhaps not in so overwhelming and dazzling a way, but perceptibly nonetheless. Something of the light given to Paul at Damascus will certainly be given to everyone who labors for the gospel. This is a light that we will perceive only if God enables us to do so. "For it is the God who said, 'Let light shine out of darkness,' who has shone in our hearts to give the light of the knowledge of the glory of God in the face of Christ Jesus. But we have this treasure in earthen vessels" (2 Cor 4:6–7).

Paul connects the image of a (fragile) vessel containing something very precious, a treasure, not with himself alone (Acts 9:15), but with all who, like him, preach the gospel. The treasure here is the knowledge of who Jesus really is, the knowledge of "the glory of God" on his human face. Those who know that they are called to bring this "treasure" or the "name" of Jesus to other human beings may, like the first witnesses to Christ, apply to themselves the promise of the risen Lord: "I am with you all days to the consummation of the world" (Mt 28:20).

QUESTIONS FOR REFLECTION

How has my vocation changed my life? Have I also experienced a comparable conversion?

Does my image of Jesus contain distortions, as that of the early Saul did?

Do I realize that the earthly Jesus and the risen Jesus are one and the same?

In his letters Paul writes of his vocation in varying ways, without exhausting it. Have I too begun to realize the riches and wealth of my vocation?

17

Called out of Darkness into Marvelous Light

*T*he vocation stories of the Old and New Testaments are exemplars in various respects. In many of their characteristic features they are typical of the way in which God calls human beings and entrusts them with a mission. But in the New Testament it is not only selected individuals but the church as a whole that is called. A good example is the community of Corinth, which Paul reminds to "consider your own call" (1 Cor 1:26). This community, which contains many poor, weak, and lowly people, persons without prestige, is an example of how God's choice ignores human ideas of worth (1 Cor 1:26–31). In principle, all in the community should think of themselves as called and as "saints" (1 Cor 1:2, 24; Rom 1:6–7). God's call is thus not limited to a special group; nor should it lead to an elitist consciousness of self.

In the New Testament God's call has three special characteristics:

(a) It is mediated through Jesus. In other words, the way in which Jesus calls human beings and binds them to himself displays a claim such as no human being, no teacher or prophet, can make, but only God. Unique too is the way in which he takes care of those who follow him and in which they have a personal closeness to him. A particular indication of this is his prayer for them (Lk 6:12; 22:32; Jn 17:9–26) and the irrevocable promise of his assistance (Mt 28:20). Today still, often in the little things of everyday life, the followers of Jesus experience his care and help.

(b) A call from God leads to participation in the mission of Jesus. His proclamation of the reign of God and his healing activity, indeed everything to which he had committed himself to the point even of giving his life—all this he puts in the hands of those who follow after him. Like him, they too act in the spirit of mercy (Mt 9:35–36) and service (Mk 10:42–45). In the gospel of John, Jesus interprets this participation by his followers in a very comprehensive sense: "As the Father has sent me, so I send you" (Jn 20:21; see 17:18). Those who are called continue this mission of Jesus through all the ages.

(c) A vocation also has Jesus himself as its object, inasmuch as the salvation he proclaims is not separated from his person. A passage in the letter to the Romans brings this out in a way that is easily remembered. All Christians, who in the midst of a groaning creation and in the sharing of one another's sufferings place their trust in God with hope and love, are called by God to share in the life and being of the risen Jesus and "to be conformed to the image *(eikôn)* of his Son" (Rom 8:28–30). Against the background of Genesis 1:26–27 (creation of human beings after the image of God), the concept of "image" contains the idea of partnership. In a comparable way, the first letter to the Corinthians says that God has called us to communion (Greek: *koinônia*) with his Son (1 Cor 1:9).

The sharing of a meal, an image rich in biblical symbolism, shows that a call given through Jesus has closeness to him as one of its purposes. In the parable of the great dinner (Lk 14:16–24) that is declined by those originally invited, it is, characteristically, "the poor, the crippled, the blind, and the lame" (v. 21) who are receptive to the call of invitation. The final solemn hymn in the Apocalypse of John (or Revelation), a book rich in hymnic texts, is followed by the beatitude: "Blessed are those who are called to the marriage supper of the Lamb" (19:9). *Call* here means "invite." The people of God in their final state are seen as the bride and wife of the Lamb. Many of the faithful answer this invitation at the celebration of the Eucharist and experience therein a special oneness with Jesus and are strengthened by him.

In another image, the people of God are compared with the

one hundred and forty-four thousand who follow the Lamb wherever he goes (Rv 14:3–4). They are at the same time the "called and chosen and faithful," who are with the Lamb and cleave to him—even in situations of conflict (17:14). Still another image (Rv 5:10; see 1:6; 20:6) describes this people as a kingdom of priests, which the people of Israel had already been destined to be at the time when the covenant was made (Ex 19:6; see Chapter 10, above). The dignity of priests derives from their having special access to the Holy One and being allowed to draw near to God himself. Through the blood of the Lamb, through the self-sacrifice of Jesus, Christians—all of them—have gained this dignity.

The first letter of Peter also connects the idea of a universal priesthood with the thought that the people of God as a whole have a vocation. This letter says to all who believe in Christ: "But you are a chosen race, a royal priesthood, a holy nation, God's own people, in order that you may proclaim the mighty deeds of him who called you out of darkness into his marvelous light" (1 Pt 2:9). The allusion to Isaiah cannot be missed: "the people whom I formed for myself so that they might declare my praise" (Is 43:21). For Christians, God's deeds have taken concrete form in what he has done for Jesus and through him, and especially in the mercy he has bestowed on us (1 Pt 2:10).

Along with the resumption of the prophetic tradition, the conviction that God remains true to himself also takes concrete form. Just as he has shown himself to be Liberator and Compassionate One from the very beginning of Israel's history, so he acts in a special way through the earthly Jesus and on into the history of the new people of God whom Jesus gathered. This fidelity of God, which is never something obvious but is an ever new wonder, forms a bridge from the vocation stories of the Old Testament, via those of the New Testament, to those of our own time.

Today still, God calls individuals and entire communities. Christians are convinced that God's call is at that same time the call of their Lord, the risen Jesus. In the perspective adopted by the first letter of Peter, there may be great differences in the missions that go with the calls, but in the final analysis they all consist in proclaiming the mighty acts of God and passing on the story of what he has done for us: how he has delivered us from all the darkness of alienation from God, dread, and broken relationships, and has called us to closeness with him, into his "marvelous light."